GHOST HUNTERS' TOOL KIT

Dinah Roseberry
Photography by
Stuart Schneider

80 Lower Valley Road • Atglen, PA 19310

Dedication

I'd like to dedicate this special oracle kit to **Carolyn Giles**, a dear friend whose intuitive Tarot and life knowledge, along with personal charm, brings me joy at every juncture. She has encouraged me to finish this project from my first mention of it and gave her blessing once completed.

Acknowledgments

I'd like to acknowledge and thank the many paranormal investigative groups, individual investigators, and intuitives who advised me during my preparation of this project.

Additional appreciation goes to Stuart Schneider, my wonderful partner, who didn't blink once when I asked him if I could use his magnificent artwork — he just said yes without even thinking about it.

Finally, a special thanks to:

The Light Beings
Beckah Boyd
Jennifer Marie Savage
John Cheek
Pete Schiffer
Peter Schiffer

Paranormal Books by Stuart Schneider
Ghosts in the Cemetery, 978-0-7643-2988-3, $19.99
Ghosts in the Cemetery II: Farther Afield, 978-0-7643-3590-7, $24.99

Paranormal Books by Dinah Roseberry
Ghosts of Valley Forge and Phoenixville, 978-0-7643-2633-2, $14.95
Cape May Haunts,, 978-0-7643-2821-3, $14.95
Spooky York, Pennsylvania, 978-0-7643-3021-6, $14.99
Spooky Creepy Baltimore County, 978-0-7643-3254-8, $14.99
Psychic Pets, 978-0-7643-3398-9, $12.99

Photographs by Stuart Schneider
Text by Dinah Roseberry, Schiffer Publishing

Copyright © 2011 Dinah Roseberry, Schiffer Publishing, LTD.

Library of Congress Control Number: 2011929365

All rights reserved. No part of this work may be reproduced or used in any form or by any means—graphic, electronic, or mechanical, including photocopying or information storage and retrieval systems—without written permission from the publisher.

The scanning, uploading and distribution of this book or any part thereof via the Internet or via any other means without the permission of the publisher is illegal and punishable by law. Please purchase only authorized editions and do not participate in or encourage the electronic piracy of copyrighted materials.

"Schiffer," "Schiffer Publishing Ltd. & Design," and the "Design of pen and ink well" are registered trademarks of Schiffer Publishing Ltd.

Designed by John P. Cheek
Type set in Trajan Pro/Old Claude LP /New Baskerville BT

ISBN: 978-0-7643-3912-7
Printed in China

Schiffer Books are available at special discounts for bulk purchases for sales promotions or premiums. Special editions, including personalized covers, corporate imprints, and excerpts can be created in large quantities for special needs. For more information contact the publisher:

Published by Schiffer Publishing Ltd.
4880 Lower Valley Road
Atglen, PA 19310
Phone: (610) 593-1777; Fax: (610) 593-2002
E-mail: Info@schifferbooks.com

For the largest selection of fine reference books on this and related subjects, please visit our website at
www.schifferbooks.com
We are always looking for people to write books on new and related subjects. If you have an idea for a book please contact us at the above address.

This book may be purchased from the publisher.
Include $5.00 for shipping.
Please try your bookstore first.
You may write for a free catalog.

In Europe, Schiffer books are distributed by
Bushwood Books
6 Marksbury Ave.
Kew Gardens
Surrey TW9 4JF England
Phone: 44 (0) 20 8392-8585; Fax: 44 (0) 20 8392-9876
E-mail: info@bushwoodbooks.co.uk
Website: www.bushwoodbooks.co.uk

Divination is not a specific, scientifically proven method that offers absolute answers. Therefore, decisions or interpretations based on the methods used here alone should be done cautiously. Life-altering decisions should always include professional assistance. The author, illustrator, publisher, and those mentioned herein take no responsibility for outcomes based on decisions or interpretations made using tools in this kit. Use with care.

Contents

Introduction	6
The Connection Between the Oracle and the Tarot	25
The Major Arcana Paranormal Tarot Deck	32
The Paranormal Investigation Deck	57
The Paranormal Client Deck	84
The Paranormal Recruitment Deck	109
The Cemetery Views	135
Dowsing	143
Conclusion	148
Appendix	149
Do's and Don'ts When Using the Kit Under Ghostly Circumstances	150
Other Ways to Use the Decks	154

INTRODUCTION

THE NEED FOR AN ORACLE IN THE PARANORMAL FIELD

First, I must come clean and tell you that I haven't been using oracles for ten or twenty years and I haven't had experience as a Tarot reader for a multitude of decades, either. I *have* dabbled and made efforts here and there to understand the varied card-reading systems that have been available over my life span. It has always amazed me how much a person could glean from them — if you understood them. Alas, in my eyes, that kind of thinking was for professionals. A lay person could not understand such a thing without mega amounts of time, energy, and frustration. (And I didn't have the time or energy and I hate feeling frustrated.)

Then some years ago, I put my foot down and decided that I was going to read Tarot cards, no matter what. So I did. Was I great? No. Was I good? Not particularly. Did people love me? Well…. Yes, they did. Did they even give me money and gifts? Yes. (Seriously, they did.) You are probably asking yourself just about now, "*How come?*" It was not because of the cards, but rather my connection to them.

Having an oracle in a scientific field is probably a frightening — or at least objectionable — arrangement for those who may feel negativity or at least irritated by the spiritual nature of things when looking for tangible evidence. Many people feel having psychics or mediums on their investigative ghost hunting teams cause haphazard results, finding that it takes away from good and true detective work. "This is not scientific study," they say, as if looking through a telescope or microscope is the only way to detect life. (I've heard 'em say it.) Alas, the time may be upon us that will show "science-minded" individuals that what they see is not always what they get. Sometimes what they *don't* see is far more interesting and enlightening with much more substance than anyone ever knew.

Cards, used in any fashion — whether in Tarot or oracles — are a method to open one's mind and to connect left and right brain thinking. Oddly, the scientific-minded often have the most difficult time with this and, though you might think that those who are comfortable using this type of system to gain the most from these cards would be the case, it may be that the opposite is true. Science-minded individuals will find that if they let their minds go, and actually empty the buzz that constantly keeps the numbers and equations busy inside them (always a good thing to be sure), they will be very good at using these cards to determine varied outcomes relating to ghost investigations and other venues they choose to find answers to. In fact, they may even slide above and beyond those who are psychic or who are already card readers. Why? Because they do indeed understand connections and connective-ness. (I know that might not be a real word, but those *in with the spirit* know exactly what I mean.)

Individuals who are already open to the concept will move forward easily, using the cards and interacting with their teammates in a fashion that will reflect a team-oriented discussion and complex organism. The mysteries will be solved. Those science individuals will revert into themselves reflecting on a journey never taken and just may be flabbergasted at the abilities that rush forth in rapid-fire succession. Low and behold, they will have a mind change. They will become believers of their own accord — *if* they give it a try. Slow and cautious at first, but soon, these high-thinking individuals will "get it!" Surprise! The need is recognized and supplied.

But Hey! Reading Cards is Evil!

One thing I have heard people say from time to time as I've worked with oracle and Tarot cards is that they are evil. They can bring in "bad things." Good religious people will be doomed for using them. The tirade goes on and on.

Yes, I do know that any tool can be misused and that is why people are so incredibly frightened of Ouija boards. "Reading cards" has come under fire as being a religious no-no as well. However, we are not using cards as a way of telling the future or past or to give us ghostly abilities. (You probably won't float around the room.)

Cards are used in this case (and in most cases if people are entirely honest) to open up the brain channels of what science calls free association or brainstorming. This technique is even taught in schools in English classes under such titles as clustering, mapping, and webbing, where one puts down a word or phrase (usually in a circle in the middle of a sheet of paper) and then the student begins to "map out" words that connect to that word, webbing further and further out until a full image is clear of the original word or phrase.

For our purposes here, we use cards to make the image of a haunting, new member, or client clear. The only difference is that you include others with your mapping and, because of that, the maps change and flow and move. The cards show that we are all different. Events — and ghostly occurrences — are all different and they change behaviors (somewhat) according to who is connecting to them.

It is not evil. It goes against no religion. It calls no evil entities.

What it does do is something similar to all brainstorming techniques: It paints a picture of an event, a person or persons (or ghost), a place, or a thing. It begins to make the person or persons involved intuitive.

Presto-chango, even *you* can be psychic.

Why Here? Why Now?

Connection

Now connection may sound complicated to someone who is looking in from the outside, but everyone deals with it on a daily basis with *some*thing. Is there an area of your home where you work better, sleep better, enjoy eating more? Do you sleep better in your own bed than one at a hotel? Do you enjoy eating more at a table or in front of a television? How about at your office? Do you become off-kilter if you are forced to move into another space to work while yours is being painted? These are all space-related connections. We can be connected to *people*, too — those who make us feel good, those who make us feel romantic, or who make us laugh. We feel connected to all kinds of things. Once you get used to the idea, you can become connected to your oracle cards. This connectedness is not something you recognize. It just happens.

I became connected to my Tarot cards. Way back in the beginning, I typed tiny little messages on little pieces of paper and then taped them on the cards — they were little cheat sheets. I was on my way. The key was to listen to what was going on in front of me and connect to them — the people — as well. The person who was talking to me had an issue, otherwise they wouldn't be talking with me. The cards had meanings. This had been established way before I'd ever had knowledge of them. My connection came from what the little pieces of paper taped to the cards said as they were applied to what the person said to me. Then a little commonsense from me was added. This is how it typically went.

I'd turn over a card.

The tiny piece of paper would say: *Pitter patter of little feet.*

In my mind, I began to connect thoughts: *Baby? Little kids? Who has little feet? What kind of little feet? My dog has little feet... My feet are big feet. This person in front of me, how big are their feet?*

I would tell the person: "I see the pitter-patter of little feet. Does that make sense to you? Baby? Little kids?" (I didn't usually ask about their feet. People already thought I was a bit *off*, why prove it?)

The other person would say: "Oh no. I was afraid of that. I think my sister might be pregnant."

I'd turn over another card.

The tiny piece of paper taped to the card would say: *Wedding bells.*

I would say to the person: "Is your sister married or planning to be?"

The person says: "Yes, she is."

I would say: "Well, this pregnancy looks like a good thing, then. I'm seeing wedding bells and that seems like a good thing. Right?" (My commonsense...)

At the same time, I was looking at the pictures on the cards to get clues and tips as she talked with me about her sister and the things going on in her life, because believe it or not, the pictures also told a story — and that story changed with each person I talked with. Simplistic? Most of the time it is.

Now let me make a note here. If this person had said her sister was not married, there may have been a different interaction and outcome. Still another interaction might have occurred if the sister was having a marriage forced upon her. The connections came from interacting with the cards and the person — becoming a conduit for the information highway of sorts. Suppose the *pitter patter of little feet* was a an animal? The possibilities depend upon who the *other* person is and what they say to you. For you, this will include clients, team members, prospective team members, and ghosts.

It all is a matter of interpretation. A short story that will never allow me to sleep at night occurred one day when I read an oracle for a lady who was having trouble in a romantic relationship. As we talked, the cards showed some violence and there was a car, so my common sense and something intuitively told me to tell her to stay away from this guy and his car. That was my intuition giving me a direct hit, but then my mind got into the middle of it and I began to put in my own two cents. "Just don't get into the car with him, whatever you do." Well, I didn't see her for a couple weeks, but when I did, she was on crutches. She limped up to me and said, "Why didn't you tell me he was going to drag me down the street on the outside of the car while I was stuck in the front window?" The lesson? Know when to shut up. Intuition will come in spurts as you brainstorm and most times not in full sentences with punctuation and explanation points.

Now back to ghosts.

What one is doing by using oracle cards during ghost investigations or within a ghost group is solving mysteries relating to that field of interest. This will be another tool at the disposal of the investigator. It might not be one that every team member will be required to use, but very definitely should be a tool that at least one member should carry and become adept with. It draws out an interior thinking process that connects two entities, two people, or any connection of the two.

Gently bringing the oracle into the tool base of the group should occur as each team member uses the oracle to see how it works. In other words, play with it. In this way, it will quickly be noted who is most comfortable with it and which members will be best to utilize it on an investigation or for other purposes within the group. It will be immediately evident from using the decks what kinds of information will be forthcoming. It's possible, too, that a member may be good with one deck, but not the others. Leave room for variations of ability or learning.

In the beginning, the same one or two team members (there should be someone to take notes or preferably recordings for the reading in case EVPs are captured) should be assigned to work with the oracle so that they become comfortable with the tool. Like any new piece of equipment, becoming accustomed to the vibrations of the tool will take some time.

Putting it Together

When creating these decks, I asked myself, when were the important times that something like this would be valuable for a team's usage? It certainly would not be easy to use by flashlight in the dark as one roamed through the basements of historic homes or abandoned prisons, cemeteries, or other ghostly locations. So what then would its purpose be?

The Investigation at a Glance

Before the Investigation

Using the oracle before the investigation can help tip the team off to any obstacles that may crop up relating to both the client and the location. It can also predict how members on the team will respond to the energy of the location if that is a concern for the team.

At the Investigation

The best time to use it when dealing with a client is on the day of the investigation, but *prior* to the start of the investigation. While the team is setting up equipment (and oftentimes when the homeowner or business people are following the team around and possibly in the way without meaning to be), this is the perfect time for one or two investigators (particularly someone who is psychically sensitive) to work with the client and the oracle deck. Information gathered at this time is not only helpful, but oftentimes provides additional important information that takes the case in a new or at least supplementary direction. Discussion of outcomes should take place with team leaders prior to the investigation to provide any new information or suggestions coming from this oracle session. You'll be surprised at how much the client may have forgotten or neglected to tell you.

During or After an Investigation

Certainly, anytime during or after an investigation, if a team member feels the need for clarification or wants to further interact with a spirit, the oracle can spur activity. Much like the K-2 meter that lights up *yes* or *no* to answer questions, the oracle can spur reactions so that it complements the K-2 or EVP practices perfectly.

Obviously, light will be needed to read the cards, but aside from that, a reading can be conducted by one person with a tape recording device used to collect ghostly answers or the K-2 answers by flashing lights. These cards can also be read while using ITC equipment.

As a Hiring Tool

Many groups have hiring practices in place for bringing new members into their groups. These usually consist of questionnaires and an interview, as well as a probationary period. The oracle has also provided good insight for this. It works wonders for drawing people out during conversation and relaxing them so that the true person comes through — much better than ink blots!

As you know, during interviews, people tend to have their best personas in place. They want the job. This is even more so for any volunteer endeavor such as joining most investigative paranormal teams (usually nonprofit entities). Having done their homework, they will have usually watched all the television shows, but they know, via literature, that most groups find the television shows "showy" and much of the time lacking some of the reality that exists. (In reality, it's not that the

> **ITC Equipment:** ITC, or Instrumental Transcommunication, is the use of modern technological devices to communicate to what is referred to as "the other side." ITC researchers operate under the assumption that various intelligent entities respond to the use of radio-based Instrumental Transcommunication devices and that the repeat communications provide enough evidence to continue researching. Other ITC technology is used to communicate with these intelligent entities; computers, telephones, video cameras, television screens, faxes, and audio recorders continually capture evidence of communication from the other side.
>
> From: ITCvoices.org

television shows lack it, it's that they only have a short period of time — one hour — to show evidence that oftentimes takes ten hours to collect. Their job includes entertainment. This is not so for a normal investigative group.)

Therefore, the interviewee knows what the interviewer is likely to ask and knows what opinions and answers should be given. When the group utilizes the oracle cards, something different happens. To begin with, the interviewer will be taken out of a normal interview session and placed into a more interactive personal interaction. Through the cards, areas will be touched upon in different and deeper ways that will bring forth a clearer picture of what the prospective member might be thinking or can offer the group.

The oracle can also be consulted prior to an interview to tip you off to any issues that you may want to touch upon. Though the oracle uses generalities, you will find that the person answering the reader will provide the specifics.

Note: Equipment Needed to Aid With Oracle Readings at an Investigation

- Tape Recorder
- K-2 Meter or EMF meter to note spirit activity (optional)
- Pen/paper for notes
- Light to read cards (artificial)
- Reading cloth to keep card area clean (this can be small — the size of a handkerchief is a good size)
- Protective stones or other protective measures that the group or individuals reading the cards uses

> **Tip:** You, too, can weed out undesirables. Let the prospective member do the talking. (Remember not to insult even if the card offers one.)

Using the Tarot

Those groups that use psychics or who have people who know how to read the Tarot on their team may find that having a Major Arcana deck (which includes 22 cards) specially dedicated to ghost hunting for other members is helpful; therefore, there is a deck included that is specifically tuned to the Majors of the Tarot. Though a Tarot reader might choose to read with his or her own card deck, opting to use this one will assist others in the group to become readers as well.

Minor Arcana cards supplied by outside sources can also be added to the Majors deck if so desired to draw more specific readings by those Tarot readers who have that ability. (The Minor Arcana cards are not included in this kit.) What I have found, though, is that if a ghost hunter does not already have a working knowledge of the Tarot, they are reluctant to learn the 78-card meanings of the full Tarot deck — that's a lot of work. This small oracle deck provides a much more concise way to connect to the Tarot for them and for psychics/Tarot readers in the group to add to the oracle by using their own personal knowledge. This deck will not intimidate.

How To Prepare the Cards

There are many ways to prepare cards for usage within a team. This mostly depends upon the type of team members who belong to the group. If you have members who already read Tarot cards or other types of cards (Oracle decks like this one or animal cards, Goddess cards, etc.), then they may have a special ritual for preparation already in place. This is also true for varied religions such as Wiccan, Shamanism, or varied Pagan studies. All are appropriate according to each belief system. Preparation is more mind over matter than anything. It deals with respect of self and of the universe and connects the team to the cards, each other, and protective sources outside us. As I mentioned earlier, these cards are not religion based, but, as with all matters dealing with unknown paranormal activity, preparation according to one's own background is important.

For a team preparation the first time the cards are introduced, at the very least, the team should come together into a circular group, handle each of the cards, discuss them and their meanings, view the cemetery scenes, and generally put their energies into the cards as a group. As new members come into the group, that new member should be able to sit with one or two of the group to have this same opportunity. This ritual should repeat about once a year. If there is a particular bad (or evil) case and you've used the cards *in any way* — whether as a clarifier or within the space of evil — the preparation or cleansing (which is the same thing as preparation with this deck) should occur again. If there is a fear that this cleansing has not been enough, the cards can be placed beneath a quartz crystal overnight. This should cleanse any negative energies. Again, look to members in the group who have experience dealing with demonology or other evil entities or situations if you think you and your cards have been exposed. Also, anyone with a knowledge of gemstones will be able to help you with clearing rituals if needed.

Tip: A pendulum can be used to clear the cards. I've also heard that some use sage, say prayers over them, leave them under the full moon, conduct a specific ritual or spell. There are many ways to do this.

Then What?

Obviously, once you've taken all the time to talk about the cards and cleanse them, you should try to keep them clean! This time I don't mean in the spiritual way, rather in an aesthetic way. Your cards should be kept in a safe place (perhaps in the box in which they came or within a special cloth or bag enclosure). Most investigators have special equipment cases, and while these are great for storing equipment, your cards will need a special case within this case — cards will scatter if they are not secured. For best results, at least at the beginning and until all members are very familiar with card meanings, it will be best to have the book with you for reference. Use a reading cloth or some other protective surface to both have a clean surface and a contrast for reading the cards, and wrap the cards with cloth when they are not in use.

How to Use the Cards

Though any card spread used for any deck (whether Tarot or oracle) is appropriate for this oracle deck, the chosen spread for ghost investigation in the early days is the *Spirit of Three*.

This is a 3-card spread, but there are three questions and answers for each card and since there are multiple uses in ghost hunting, there are endless possibilities.

> Oracle Sessions should (for best results) be tape-recorded and cards read aloud. Chances of the spirits becoming directly involved with the reading are high and EVPs are often captured. It is true, however, that spirits will also respond to the cards if someone reads to themselves. However, this does not help the group investigation in most cases.

The Questions:

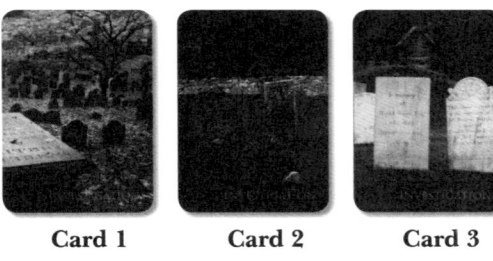

Card 1   **Card 2**   **Card 3**

The deck we will use to demonstrate will be the Investigation Deck. As you lay down the cards, always lay them in the above fashion in a 1, 2, 3 sequence. Then repeat a second layer on top the first three and then a third layer on top the second layer, so that you have three layers of three cards. (Note: I have found that at times, having three layers may take too much time. Depending on the time you wish to spend, make the decision of the number of cards ahead of time.)

The easiest labels (and the most well-known) for the card piles are always: **Past, Present, Future.**

An easy example for a ghost investigation may be as follows: An old house seems to be occupied by a ghost that materializes by a window. She pulls back the drapes, appears to cry, and then disappears. (I know, I just pulled it out of the air...)

The cards are spread out on the table and three are spread in the *Spirit of Three* layout.

You would take the Card 1 pile and read all three cards together as the *Past* linking the meanings together. Suppose the cards in the Card 1 pile were:

Card 0 (meaning) Starting Over
Card 3 (meaning) Creation
Card 8 (meaning) Decisions

(Note: The meanings I'm showing will be given to you later on.)

What does the past indicate as you connect these three cards and think of the woman at the window? As a team, consider this. Think about what the client may have told you. Was there a decision to be made a long time ago. Did someone start over or feel that the only way out of a situation was to leave to begin again? Was something created. Could a child be related? Was there a baby? Was the creation a marriage or a love? Did someone start a new life, though a decision had to be made once and for all — even though there was so much sadness? Talk about it out loud, *slowly*, so that there is space for EVP interaction.

The same method is used for Card Pile 2 and Card Pile 3. A picture begins to form as the team discusses how what the cards say may fit in with what the evidence suggests and what the client has said. Or does it? Is something missing? Is one or the other wrong? Do you need to ask more questions? With the cards, this is possible.

You may choose new cards for the three piles and again go through the answers and discussions in the same manner, but now there is the opportunity to assign the three piles three new questions before you lay down the cards. The next question for pile 1 might be instead of Past: *Why is the woman so sad?* (Any questions that apply can be added to replace the present and future card piles.)

If you wish and if it is appropriate, you can bring in the client because, oftentimes, they bring a fresh perspective that you may have no way of understanding. Sometimes, this kind of "brainstorming" (because that is really what this is...) will bring out facts or clues that they've forgotten to tell you. It may also loosen things that you or your team have seen or perceived on another level that have gone unrealized.

MORE ABOUT MAKING YOUR OWN SPREAD

Don't be surprised to find that a preconceived out-of-the-box spread does not work for your session. You may find that as you lay a card down, you (or someone on your team) are spurred immediately into talking about that card without thinking about it's "Past, Present, Future" location. It happens more often than you might think.

So, once you've tried the easy three-card spreads, you can move on to making your own

20 Introduction

spread—or making no spread. This is imperative for ghost investigations. Why? Because every investigation is different. Every client is different. Every recruit is different. Yes, you may have spreads that are beginning jump-off points, but after that, you will find out very quickly that plain and standard spreads telling the past, present, and future offer little help to you. Sound complicated? It's not. All you need is a list of questions or themes that are related to the case. First, you begin with your jump-off list. What is a jump-off list? It's merely a listing of questions you can use if you can't think of a way to begin.

JUMP-OFF QUESTIONS

1) What is the situation?

2) What is the main obstacle?

3) What in the past happened?

4) What in the recent past happened?

5) What is happening now?

6) What will happen in the immediate future?

7) What will the final outcome be?

8) What message must I have?

The above questions give you a jump-off point. There are eight questions, and they require eight cards. If you choose two questions, they require two cards, three require three, and so on.

The first thing to know is whether these questions deal with the topic of an investigation, a recruitment, or a client. Can you see by choosing one of these three topics how the answers might change? Lay out eight cards (or the number you choose) from the appropriate deck to begin your reading. Each question and answer builds upon the one prior. For example, once you read what the situation entails, the obstacle that comes next would be an obstacle for the situation, and so on.

It doesn't stop there, though. Once you have the answers in front of you, there may be other questions that are spurred on from the question you asked. You now can identify those questions and lay down more cards as answers or clarifiers to them. **The only caution is, you must identify the questions you'd like to ask *prior* to laying down the cards (otherwise it's kinda like cheating... you'd be forcing the answer you want to a question you're about to ask).** You might also like to pick up the cards you've laid down and reshuffle between each set of questions since the decks are small. (See the section regarding the Major Arcana deck to find out how to use those cards as *wild cards* in one of the other three decks, bringing the number of cards from 22 to 44 and doubling the possible outcomes.) It may be best for someone to write down your new questions prior to reshuffling if you have a poor memory. Any number of questions or topics are appropriate. This gives the universe time to insert itself into the deck.

You will find that once you have identified what your jump-off questions will be, you should be ready to consider more questions for each situation. Can you see how the new questions for a ghost investigation in a private home might be different from those in a cemetery? You will also find that new questions may be determined by the answers found from the jump-off questions. Every investigation will be different, therefore every card reading, jump-off list, and outcome will also be different, as they will reflect your investigation and provide another aspect to your evidence.

> **Tip:** Whenever you read cards with people outside your group (clients or prospective members), you may bring up cards that have negative connotations. You will need to be careful how you present this material in open forum. You are in the public and should refrain from boxing yourself or your team into an uncomfortable corner. Reputations are at stake.

Obviously, if you are trying to find out if a new member candidate is honest and a card comes up that tells you that he or she lacks honesty, you should not say: *This card tells me that you may be dishonest.*

Instead, you might ask:

> *How do you feel about honesty? If you wanted a client to believe you and your evidence was not as great as you'd hoped, but you really had seen something, would you tell them that the evidence supported what you saw 100 percent even though it didn't?*

It's then that you would draw the person into a discussion of ethics. After they have answered, you will have a better understanding of how he or she will react on the team and whether the dishonesty card is a severe issue or one you can deal with.

The next card might say that the person has a positive outlook, is open-minded, and good at reviewing evidence. You can hook it to the prior card by saying:

> *Do you think that you are good at reviewing evidence? Do you think that you put a positive swing on things sometimes if the case deems it necessary? What if someone else stretched the truth, what would you do? When?*

This of course is a simplistic example; you will find that the cards go deeper and may cover ground that you've not thought of before. It's a really handy tool to have at your disposal.

> ## An Investigation Caution
> One of the first experiments using the Investigation deck during an EVP session occurred at the very haunted Gettysburg Battlefield Bed and Breakfast in Pennsylvania. It was my intention to use a regular three-card spread and to include the group historian and myself as test subjects within one of the haunted bedrooms.
>
> It became quickly evident that a normal three-card spread with dedicated questions from the jump-off list or even a Past/Present/Future spread were not necessary. When I laid down one card, I began to talk and because both the historian and I were familiar with the haunts of this Gettysburg location, we were able to begin our discussion right away. (As you know, in a normal investigation, the group usually

knows something about what is happening prior to arrival.) We merely laid down three cards, talked, and asked questions. It worked splendidly. The questions had much more depth than our normal EVP session questions (or compared to during any other EVP session I'd witnessed). The ground covered in the three cards, with an additional three cards atop those, totaled thirty minutes time — a reasonable (if not too long) time for an EVP session that was quite intense. We were both pleased.

However, upon listening to the replay of the recording, there was one major issue that arose, which I'd like to pass on to you as firm advice. Because the cards were so compelling with the ability to pull questions from us for the spirits, we had not left what I consider enough gap time for the spirit to answer. While it is true that oftentimes spirits will talk during, behind, or over the human speaker, it is still the preferred method to leave 10 to 15-second intervals of blank air time for spirits to use. We routinely, during this practice session, moved too quickly along. It may have worked just as well to only use three cards in this particular session.

Note that each session you hold will be as different as each investigation and will require varied numbers of cards and that they can be used in any number of ways. You will find your comfort zone as you move forward.

A good "check" might be to have a third party not involved in the card reading to be a time watcher. That person can signal when the human voices should stop and start or if you are moving too quickly along, thereby giving the card readers gestures so that they can concentrate on the reading and not on the timing.

As a side note, we did not get an EVP, but in the hallway outside the bedroom our motion sensor camera caught a light anomaly that no one can seem to identify.

The Connection Between the Oracle and the Tarot

With open-ended questions spurred by the cards, you have your prospective member talking without insulting him or her by, for example, accusing them of being dishonest. (Hmmmm... Again, this sounds like a job interview — and in a way it is, isn't it?)

Because my beginnings in card reading came from the Tarot, and because many ghost groups incorporate members who have experience with Tarot as a sideline interest, I decided that this oracle should benefit not only the members who had no experience with card reading, but also those who loved the Tarot. Therefore, each oracle card meaning is attached to a Major Arcana card of the Tarot and that Tarot number is indicated on the card in the upper right hand corner. It is appropriate for a seasoned Tarot reader to use that information (or not). In that way, anyone can benefit from these decks at any level. If you don't know the Tarot, you don't need to use that number. Once you understand the Oracle and have used it consistently, you can add the numbers in at any time, especially if you decide you would like to learn more about them.

Take out the cards and follow along

In this companion book, both the name of the equivalent Tarot card and its number are displayed as well as the oracle keyword explanation.

The oracle keywords easily identify meanings so that a reader can quickly begin to understand the cards with minimum need for the booklet.

The meanings are not long and cumbersome; rather they are common sense and, with very few words, any ghost enthusiast will be able to apply them to the varied investigative situations that arise.

The main keyword always refers to a universal meaning that goes with the Tarot and the number.

The words in smaller font are the words that go deeper into the ghost world meanings. (*These are the potatoes and vegetables to the Tarot meat.*)

The book goes a bit deeper, advising separate meanings for investigations, understanding clients, interview sessions for new members, and of course, keywords.

Using the deck and book will eventually allow the readers in your group to commit the meanings to memory if desired.

This is very helpful and opens up an entire realm of discovery, but even that is not an issue because the keywords on the cards are detailed enough for spurring the mind.

CARD MEANINGS

The 4 decks — Major Arcana, Client, Investigation, and Recruitment — each have labels and color codes that will show the reader the difference in topic as follows:

Major Arcana – Purple
Client – Blue
Investigation – Orange
Recruitment – Rust

Each card will have Major Arcana Tarot Keyword text and an identification number that will be the main drivers for the cards throughout the four decks and those Keywords will be shown on the card in a larger font. These words will be the most important keys and will give you the biggest clues when brainstorming the answers to your questions. You will have the most leeway to consider what you are experiencing and how it applies to a particular clue word from the card. These clues are also the broadest when it comes to determining the issues you face.

The Connection Between the Oracle and the Tarot 27

There will be specific clue meanings that are both different and closely aligned with the four topics (client, investigation, recruitment, and Tarot) via the other information listed on the cards in smaller type.

The larger-sized Keywords and associated number will be reflected throughout each deck as a connection to the Tarot, which is in direct communication with the universe. In this way, the decks could (and should) be mixed, if the need arises. Or each deck could stand alone.

Please note that the smaller deck words may be more explanatory in the book due to space constraints on the card. For the first several investigations you may need to refer to the book to look into deeper meanings from the paragraphs that detail each card if you become "stuck." (What I have found during the experimental investigations however was that no one was ever stuck. Words just seemed to flow. This was always due to appropriate preparation for the investigation, client interview, or client discussion. No one I worked with during this time acted "on the lamb." This was a fine testimony to professionalism and how it eases the addition of new equipment to a group.)

> **What did she say?** It works really well if you combine the Major Arcana deck with any of the other decks. Not only does it give you more cards, but you have deeper meanings. The Tarot cards are the Wild Cards!

The reader will know which Keyword was hooked to which faction of the decks based on the border colors. (Mixing decks is recommended only after the reader has a working knowledge of each individual deck. It minimizes confusion when learning. Truth be told, after using each deck one time, you should be ready to go!) Do note though that these decks are specifically slanted to the world of ghost hunting and may be difficult to use in any other mainstream venue.

One thing to remember in any type of card reading is not to discount your own feelings as you pick a card. At times, you may find that what you feel is in complete conflict with what message the card gives. This means something. As

28 The Connection Between the Oracle and the Tarot

with all normal investigative procedures in the ghost world, if you feel it or think it, say it — out loud. There still should be no whispering. We are all taught that thoughts and feelings have precedence and value during the investigative process. It is no different in this circumstance. You will find that Tarot readers often have this happen to them and they will include these impressions in their readings, recognizing that the universe is sending them an intuitive message that must hook to the meaning of the card in some fashion. Don't doubt yourself. In most cases, someone in the room (or on the other side in this situation) will give a clue as to what the connective issue is.

Tip: If you think it, say it. It could mean something. Keep an open mind.

A Special Note About Reversed Cards

If during layouts, cards are drawn and laid out in a reversed pattern, take the upright meaning and add a caution to it.

For example, the first card or the number 0 [zero] of any of the decks means "**Starting Over**." If this card is reversed, the general meaning (upright) would be:

The residual repetition of the haunting occurring over and over again in a loop — starting over and over.

If reversed, a caution is added:

This loop is not providing the lesson needed for the spirit. It is possible that this spirit may not be able to move on after all.

While We're At It...

Just for fun, lets take this card, *Starting Over,* and put it into practice at an experimental session to give you an idea of how the brainstorming in a group might go.

The card, *Starting Over,* is turned over.

Jane: Starting over. Okay, this investigation has people seeing a soldier walking into a wall every night at sundown.

Tom: And he looks back just before he disappears into the wall. It's residual.

Jane: What's on the otherside of that wall?

Pause 15 seconds

Tom: The card was reversed and that would mean that while he keeps starting over every night, he's not getting it. Whatever he's doing, he's not at peace. Who or what are you looking for?

Pause 15 seconds

Jane: Where is he coming from? Where is he going to? When he looks back, people say he looks sad... Why are you sad? Did you see somebody die?

Tom: Of course someone died (laugh). It's the Civil War! Which side are you on?

Pause 15 seconds

Jane pulls another card.

Jane: It's the *Power* card. Look at this, the picture is a Gettysburg cemetery. Does that have any meaning to you? Were you buried at this cemetery? Where were you buried?

Tom: The power card says that the ghost is powerful and may be angry, but this soldier doesn't look angry....

Pause 15 seconds

Jane: Maybe someone else is. Someone on the other side of the wall. You know there's really no wall back in the day... Or it also means there's a message. Could it be a message? Do you have a message?

Pause 15 seconds

[An EMF meter lights up]

Tom: You hit it! He has a message for someone and he's here. The card says a male and a message for the *Power* card and it must be linked with him repeating something over and over...

Pause 15 seconds

Jane: But a residual isn't an intelligent haunting. How can there be a message? A different spirit must be here, too. Let's pull another card.

Do you see how the use of the cards can be more interesting and pull out more questions than just using a list of ordinary *What is your name/How old are you* questions? Are they on the right track? Maybe. Maybe not. Will answers show in the form of EVPs on their recordings? Possibly. How would the use of ITC equipment fair with the cards? Really well, we've found. There are lots of opportunities for card usage.

(See The Paranormal Investigation Deck Chapter for the protocol for setting up a card reading during an investigation.)

> **Tip:** If you have experience with Tarot and find that you have more insight on reverse cards and know other ways to interpret them, feel free to do so. Make sure your team knows that you will be doing this. The universe, after all, knows this already and has made allowances for it, but explanations do need to be made to your team members.

Protection

Before you consult the cards in any fashion, it is advisable that you set a form of protection in place. Remember that any form of divination can summon those of a nature that you do not want — even if this is just brainstorming for you, this is still being accomplished in a ghost zone. This is particularly the case when investigating paranormal phenomena and is not something that you should forget or take lightly.

Prior to any usage then, someone in the group should be responsible for putting the protection of the team in place. (It is also true that each individual, too, should be responsible for his or her own protection and should add a prayer/ritual to his or her own religious/protective aspect to the measures of the group.) There should be a grounding ceremony with protection conducted that covers all involved. Most groups already have this kind of ritual in place. If not, it is best to determine the varied beliefs of your group and prepare such measures as they may be different for each group and each person.

My particular protective ritual involves invoking the Christ Consciousness and places a white light of protection around myself and those with me. My grounding attaches me to the earth via roots that go to the core of the earth and my arms raised to the heavens to the white light, thereby connecting me to heaven and earth.

The Major Arcana Paranormal Tarot Deck

The Major Arcana Paranormal Tarot Deck

The Major Arcana cards are the *Wild Cards* of the paranormal kit. They can be used right along with any of the other three decks, thereby increasing each of those decks from 22 cards to 44. They should be shuffled and reshuffled each time the other decks are shuffled and pulled from as desired.

For those in the group who read the traditional Tarot, this deck will hold special significance as there are specific meanings that have been handed down from times of old that can be added. The meanings here reflect that, but are slanted to accommodate situations arising in the paranormal world.

Tip: The Paranormal Tarot Deck can be used with any other deck. It can be used as a stand alone deck as a clarifier or it can be mixed in with another deck as you shuffle. *(A clarifier is an additional card that is laid down overtop a card whose meaning is unclear in the situation. The new card on top helps to clarify that meaning.)*

Major Arcana Paranormal Tarot Deck Meanings

0
The Fool

Keyword: Starting Over

Repeating patterns, understanding the past; lessons learned, possible journey

It's time to begin again — even if the beginning has happened over and over and over again. The spirit (or ghost) in this situation could be residual and repeating a pattern that indicates its need to understand something that has happened in the past. It is not aware of anything but the repeating nature of the lesson. How often must the scene be repeated?

Unknown. This is something that no one on this side has a true concept about. The higher soul has much to learn from a past life in this particular situation and the only way to truly understand some lessons is by residually reliving the moment or circumstances until the lesson is fully digested. Then that soul can move on. (Maybe — or it may continue to repeat; the actual proof of residual hauntings and their meanings do not exist.)

If there is no indication of a residual haunting, the card could also lean towards a journey. This card will always take hints from the cards around it, for the ghost or spirit here is a traveler and the lessons are almost always reflected in situations hinted at elsewhere in the reading. Oftentimes, you will be able to see those indicated in this card moving about in *all* the other cards, though cleverly hidden or appearing to run away from you or something it is uncomfortable with.

Sometimes there are jokes involved, fun, happy times, and you may hear stories of a trickster ghost.

Cemetery View: The Old South Church Cemetery, Bergenfield, New Jersey

1
MAGICIAN
Keyword: Energy

Deliver message or focused person; charged situation

The spirit or ghost here is gathering energy in every way possible. It has a message and is using all resources — including the team at hand — to gather its power so that the energy can be directed towards the message. The message and perceived magick in this card is serious and not to be played with or dismissed, for a great clue will be lost if this happens.

There is another possibility though. The ghost may have been an energetic and very focused person in life and is just projecting that in death, too.

Deciding which will depend on the other cards surrounding this one, but regardless, there is a charged feeling around this situation.

It is possible that good, solid EMF readings can be collected if this card is drawn.

Cemetery View: The Woodside Cemetery, Dumont, New Jersey

2
High Priestess
Keyword: Cycles

Psychic experience; intuitive, disappearing ghost

The ghosts or spirits here are very aware of the cycles surrounding life and death. They look from the otherside into this realm and at the team with both curiosity and quiet understanding. They know that we tend to try to rush cycles on this side, but this is something that just cannot be accomplished no matter how hard we try. These ghosts are those who seem to look through us or right at us and then disappear before our eyes. We know that a psychic experience has occurred for us, but it has gone and left no proof on any of the science equipment.

When this card arises there is a key to be found that opens the door to a mystery. Most likely that mystery has to do with an intuitive feeling that someone in the group has felt but not put into words to the others on the team. That person should step forward now — even if the thoughts seem strange or crazy. Spit it out!

Cemetery View: The Woodside Cemetery, Dumont, New Jersey

3
THE EMPRESS
Keyword: Creation

Unfinished business, manipulation; possibly negative or may be creative

This spirit has unfinished business: Something started in life has not been completed. The creation of the right kind of haunting allows this ghost to manipulate a household, person, family, or even animal into assisting with the problem. This could be as little as a piece of jewelry lost, needing to be found or something else that reflects a positive outcome. It can show a productive, creative spirit.

In life, the spirit may have been close to nature or a very attentive parent. Carrying those traits to the otherside may have brought forth a nurturing ghost.

It can also include cases where demonology is at the forefront. The negative cases can be identified fairly quickly and should, just as quickly, be dealt with by bringing in the appropriate investigator — a demonologist. (See *Demons and Demonology in the 21st Century* by Katie Boyd for advice if this is the case).

Cemetery View: Parkesburg Cemetery, Pennsylvania

4
THE EMPEROR
Keyword: Power

Strong presence, throwing energy around

The ghost in this situation was either powerful in life and is now throwing around its energy in death, or had no power in life and has an angry power now that is causing a negative haunting.

However, not all ghosts indicated with this card are showing angry power. Some just have a strong presence, meaning they were — or are — very sure, very certain, very proud of themselves. This most likely applied to their lives on earth and has followed them into death.

The spirit involved is usually male, or at the very least someone involved needs to get a message to a father figure or male mate.

Cemetery View: Gettysburg, Pennsylvania

5
HIEROPHANT
Keyword: Believing

Trusted person, understands right and wrong

The person who is involved with this card is a true believer, not necessarily in the paranormal, but in doing what is right. There is belief in right and wrong, good and evil, high road and low road. This is a person to be trusted to do what is right for everyone involved and is good to have on a team.

There are also prayers around this card or someone who has an incredible faith and knows that such faith will be required for a mystery to be solved. It may be a team member, but more likely the client who feels heartache or sympathy for the spirit who seems trapped in this world.

Cemetery View: Saugerties Cemetery, New York

6
LOVERS
Keyword: Union

*Romantic or special friends;
love by sea disappears*

A romantic union or special friendship is indicated here; possibly a separation of friends or lovers through the death of one. The love is still there and the pain is so debilitating that the one on this side feels devastated all the time. The anomaly may include sweet or synchronistic signs like special songs on the radio or flower petals when there are no flowers, etc.

This ghost may also be seen as one of the apparitions that waits by the shoreline looking out to sea, one presumes for a love lost, only to disappear before a watcher's eyes — a residual conflict unresolved.

However, not all unions for this card need to be about love. This could be indicative of someone who has to make a hard choice between one thing or another before a union can take place.

Cemetery View: Good Hill Cemetery, Kent, Connecticut

7
The Chariot

Keywords: Conflict & Resolution

Opposing forces, carrying out plans, victory

This card is about opposing forces: mostly that there is a conflict with a spirit or around a haunting, but that there is a full resolution, too. It talks about appropriate preparation and carrying out plans exactly right, with victory following.

Looking deeper into the card, you will note that this card talks of someone coming to the rescue — the knight in shining armor, the "Ripley" to the Marines (from the movie *Aliens*).

Someone does their best work under pressure: Is this a team member or the client — or is the spirit/ghost working overtime to get a message to you?

Cemetery View: Green-Wood Cemetery, Brooklyn, New York

8
Justice
Keyword: Decisions

*Difficult for ghost, intelligent haunting;
clues no sense, ask what/why*

This shows that a ghost or spirit must do something that is often very difficult to do: make decisions. It is not to say that they are not free to do so on the otherside because they are, but to make a decision that affects this side and therefore brings forth hauntings are looked upon as very serious. This does not include residual hauntings where the spirit is trying to learn something based on its own behavior. It deals with intelligent hauntings where that ghost or spirit has made its presence known for a specific purpose that affects humans on this side.

Sometimes clues are left for humans and those are often maddening when they seem to make little sense. However, if not an intelligent haunting, this card could indicate a person or ghost involved in the justice field — police, judge, lawyer, or anyone upholding the law. Either way, there is a decision in the air that has to be made, making the "what" and the "why" important questions to ask and investigate.

Cemetery View: Green-Wood Cemetery,
Brooklyn, New York

9
HERMIT
Keywords: Seeking Truth

Visions, lost, intimidated by equipment; listen in your mind

The ghost or spirit wishes to converse with you, but will only do so through visions or non-scientific means. It feels lost and alone and longs for the warmth of a real person and is intimidated by EMF meters and video screens. Put them down and turn them off. Listen to your gut and your feelings. That little voice in your head that sounds like your own but is saying alien words is the spirit — not you.

Have you seen feathers in your home prior to your investigation? This is notification that this spirit knows you are coming and will "light" your way if you allow your mind to be open, but you must allow your mind to journey on without the devil on your shoulder crying for scientific signs. This may be a test of strength for you.

Cemetery View: Green-Wood Cemetery, Brooklyn, New York

10
Wheel of Fortune

Keyword: Fate

Risks, message long overdue (positive)

The spirit reflected when this card appears has a measure of fate in play — it's meant to be. There were risks in life and now there seems to be the same kinds of risks on the otherside, but these are things that those on this side cannot fathom. Still, it's like a wheel that turns and the risks disappear as the positive signs of luck roll forward.

At this time, the spirit comes to this side with a message long overdue of a positive nature for the client. It could be a personal message from a spirit the client knows or a totally unknown spirit sent by angels. (This spirit will not bring messages of the negative nature when the wheel reflects risk and will absorb that pessimism.)

Any haunting related to this card has positive features and will give a favorable slant to nearby cards.

Cemetery View: Green-Wood Cemetery, Brooklyn, New York

11
STRENGTH
Keyword: Telepathy

Calm, animal connection; intuitive answers

The ghost or spirit relating to this card is specifically involved with a calm demeanor and an intuitive connection to the client. This spirit projects its messages intuitively into the mind of those trying to connect. Very little will be picked up on EVP, though there may be EMF activity.

There may also be an animal connection to this card. It could mean an animal on the otherside or this side, or even an animal communicator in your group or one known to the client. Be sure to ask clients: What animals are involved in their daily lives? How are they affected by the haunting? Have they heard animal sounds from the otherside?

Cemetery View: Green-Wood Cemetery, Brooklyn, New York

12
THE HANGED MAN
Keyword: Crossroads

Move or stay, may take team's advice

The ghost here has to decide whether to continue in the same situation or move into another direction, possibly away from an intelligent haunting. Sometimes, the spirit will take the advice of an investigative team, a client, or a psychic counselor if it sees it as good, feasible advice and if it feels that there is trust involved (sometimes there is a fear of trusting the living so the team may have to be on their best behavior). This might not be so easy if there is still a mystery to solve or a test to pass. There is a fear of letting go for the spirit and of not wanting to make a sacrifice. Ultimately, the decision must come from the spirit itself, just as our decisions must come from our own being.

Cemetery View: Green-Wood Cemetery, Brooklyn, New York

13
DEATH

Keyword: Change

Strong change; time of grieving

A strong card about change. A spirit's change, a client's change, a situational change, or a resisting of change. Any kind of change can be indicated by this card, but rest assured the change will affect the client and the spirit specifically.

It could also be a time of grieving for the client as the spirit must stand by, unable to move on, because of the remorse that has been left behind. Look to the cards around this one for clues about the kind of change involved and who the change may include.

This, too, is one time that the Death card can indeed be about death. Be sure to look deeper than that, though, because such an obvious interpretation will not usually bring you the answers you need.

Cemetery View: Boothbay, Maine

14
Temperance
Keyword: Miracles

Creative message that feels like a miracle

This card brings miracles along with the paranormal: Is the client waiting for something wonderful to happen that involves the otherside? Is he or she waiting for a message or has a spell been cast?

The spirit either comes with a message in a creative way or it was a creative person in life; either way, it feels to the client as though a miracle has occurred and that life has now transformed into a new amazing place.

You may find that though someone wants to know everything they can about the spirits or ghosts involved, they do not want those entities to cross over — rather they want them to stay and either be "part of the family" or an enhancement to a business. This is a time not to convince the client to take particular steps that agree with the team's philosophy, but to ask themselves what is best for the spirit.

Cemetery View: Boothbay, Maine

15
THE DEVIL
Keyword: Trap

Warning, negative haunting, out of options, danger; poltergeist if teen about

When this card is seen, there is cause for warning. The haunting could be negative and the client may be trapped — held as a slave in fear and unable to break free from an onslaught of negative anomalies. It appears that nothing has worked and the client has run out of options. The spirit is mocking and dangerous. This could indicate a demon presence.

On the other hand, it could also indicate poltergeist activity, especially if a young teen is living at the residence. Then the anomalies may seem violent, but would stop once the teen was removed.

Look at the cards around this one to see if there are other messages that could have a negative twist, as this card may be a warning relating to another message you have received during the reading. The team should keep a wary eye out in case there is foul play involved: could be a spirit wanting to disrupt their equipment, give false readings, or trick them in some way into giving a report to the client that is full of errors and therefore misguidance.

Cemetery View: Fallsington, Pennsylvania Cemetery

16
Tower
Keyword: Electricity

Shock, impulsive idea, storms

Electrical impulses, lightning from the sky, shock, storms — a very scary card for most. This is one card where the reverse has a more positive message than the upright. There may be interference with electrical equipment or someone may have been struck by lightning.

It could, though, mean a very impulsive idea (that could be a good thing) or a shocking inspiration. Still… Be careful when you see this card. You might want to look around for a rubber mat to stand on!

Cemetery View: Fallsington, Pennsylvania Cemetery

17
STAR

Keywords: High Hopes

Shining Star, potential, right place at right time

A shining star comes to light with this card and the wondrous waters of life are poured down upon your head — you can do no wrong. A star you are! High hopes! Great potential! You are at the right place at the right time. There is someone who sighs when you are near. There are so many things going in your favor all at once. If there were a caution, it would be that of burnout. So many things happening!

Now, are these things part of the investigation? Or are you bringing something in? Could this be the ghost having feelings of wonder? That is possible. Everyone on the team should take notice of any soft breathing in their ears, for it just may be an anomaly.

Cemetery View: Jerome, Arizona Cemetery

18
MOON
Keyword: Instincts

Instinct, schedules; an end to something

This is a card of instinct and schedules and calendars. There's a time for everything and everything in its own time, but routines can become interrupted and schedules thrown off if one is not careful. Something could come to an end.

Also what of the creatures of the night: those that howl at the moon or hide behind dark shadows? Is something hiding? Do your instincts warn you of something ... Or do they invite you forward? The moon has always had its mysteries and here there is no difference. Paranormal activity runs high and visibly when this card shows.

Cemetery View: Jerome, Arizona Cemetery

19
Sun

Keywords: Free Will

Personal freedom, free spirits, changing seasons

Personal freedoms, unchained movement, and free spirits are part of the intrigue of this card. Open-minded thinking and feeling the ability to move forward without the curbing of ideas by others is highlighted. In another way, nature, too, is involved. Seasons that come and go in a positive way — a welcoming fashion, where one enjoys what each change in the world around him or her sees, and participates in, is brought life.

The spirit, too, has free will. It may be ready to move on now or it may even be gone prior to the team arriving. Either way, the client will be happy at the ending of this investigation if it continues in this fashion. It's a sunny day in the neighborhood.

Cemetery View: Jerome, Arizona Cemetery

20
Judgment
Keywords: Final Decisions

*Destiny defined, outcomes;
questions answered by surrounding cards*

This card defines one's destiny and helps with final decisions. It answers the outcomes of questions that relate to critical or important questions. Those questions may be the ones asked out loud to those around you or they could just as easily be questions asked internally as you study a situation. Decisions and answers. When this card is pulled, the answer to your question — or maybe even the question itself — can be found in the cards surrounding the card.

Be careful though; it's possible that you are being judged as well. Those on the otherside have the ability (if involved in an intelligent haunting) to think about your process and your goals. They can help or hinder you. This would be a time to remember the respect rule. Do not taunt.

Cemetery View: Boothbay, Maine

21
WORLD

Keywords: Rebirth

Reincarnation, learning more lessons; circle of life

The world indicates a turning of life. It does not mean death, but rather rebirth or returning, as in reincarnation. Coming back to learn more lessons. To move towards finishing lessons and beginning still more new lessons. A vast circle of life. There could be both residual and intelligent haunts related to this card.

Someone in the group — either on this side or the otherside — is on the schoolhouse Earth. The team can be the teachers or the students. Your clients may be able to see that distinction more clearly than you right now. Ask them.

Cemetery View: Edgecomb, Maine

The Paranormal Investigation Deck

Using the Investigation Deck

EVP Sessions

The most exciting way to use the Investigation Deck is during an Electronic Voice Phenomena (EVP) session or the "silent vigil" as some of us call it. In these cases, investigators settle down into a quiet mode, usually with video recorders running, always with voice recorders running, and sometimes with Electromagnetic Field (EMF) equipment registering any ghostly phenomena in the area. There are questions asked aloud in the room with ten to fifteen seconds of quiet intervals between, giving the spirits time to interact by imprinting their sounds onto the available equipment. Sometimes the voices can be heard at the sitting, but most times, any such communication will be heard only later once the voice recorder or video recording is played back. It is then when sounds from the otherside are identified.

Conducting a reading with the cards during one of these EVP sessions is the ideal time to invite spirit communication. (Refer to the The Connection Between the Oracle and Tarot to review a sample reading.) As you shuffle the cards, announce to the spirits what you are doing and how you'd like them to respond. Advise them that their interaction with what the cards are saying will help you determine what their messages to you or the client might be, how you might help them, or any other point they might like to convey.

When reading during an EVP, it is wise to go much more slower than you would in any other kind of reading. Leave periods of silence between cards and statements. Ask questions of the spirit. Allow others in the room to participate as well. All these things will spur the spirit into the conversation that will be picked up on your voice recordings.

You may find that the first few times, the reading may feel awkward and that the voices you'd hoped for do not record. Keep trying. The spirits can oftentimes feel the discomfort and may choose not to participate because of it. Once you get the hang of it, you will find that some very interesting moments will arise. It is pertinent to note, though, that this kind of communication works only for intelligent hauntings and not for residual. Residual spirits are not aware of your presence nor do they hear you asking questions. Only those wishing to interact with you, or who have a curiosity about what you are doing, will respond.

Of course, this does not explain cannon explosions or other kinds of noises heard during these times. Are they residual? Are they responding to those reading the cards? This is unknown. It is merely another anomaly question.

Before or After an Investigation

Using the cards before or after an investigation can serve several purposes. Before, it can open the investigation, loosen team members, and focus them on certain aspects of the upcoming case. Closing the investigation, it can wind things down, keep any spirits from attaching to group members, and point out things to focus on for reports.

Make sure each reading after an investigation is ended with a closing prayer/ritual to formally conclude the investigation. This is for your protection. Please include the client and any standing observers in this ritual — and don't forget to advise the spirits listening that they are *not* invited to leave with anyone.

The Paranormal Investigation Deck Meanings

0
Equivalent Tarot: The Fool

Keywords: Starting Over

Stay in forefront, strong views; sacrifice may need to be made

How this investigation will affect you or your team personally:

You will find out very quickly that you have strong views about this case and this is a good thing, because to get to the bottom of

the "mystery," it's going to take true believers. There may even be a sacrifice you have to make if you back away to let others take on roles of leadership. You really need to be in the forefront this time. This means one leader should step forward. If that has not been decided, please do so now for the sake of the investigation.

The best thing to do is to review everything you know about this case again, right before you start the investigation with the entire team to make sure that you have not left anything out or if someone has anything to add. If you are already into the investigation, stop and count off the facts you know and those you only suspect.

If there is an entity involved in this case, it is a frivolous one. It enjoys tripping up investigators, or anyone else it can, just for the fun of it. This is not to say that you are looking at a negative haunting. It's more like "a good time was had by all" in the spirit's eyes, which doesn't always make for the best investigation.

Still, it's a starting point, and you do have to start someplace.

Cemetery View: Sleepy Hollow Cemetery, Long Island, New York

1
Equivalent Tarot: Magician

Keyword: Energy

*Focus to move through case easily;
step up to make difference*

How this investigation will affect you or your team personally:

The energy reflected in this card affects you, and every member on the team, just as it does the spirit. For (the person reading the cards), it is a positive experience. Even if there are problems with the investigation, you will have the focus to move through them easily. You are ready to "step up to the plate" and make a difference. Look around; are there others who feel that way?

When this card is pulled, there are decisions about the investigation to be made and you will find that someone in the group has an intuitive idea of what the answers should be. Go with it, for this is a good time to trust the gut, even if it seems like a strange idea. There is also sexual energy available — it is probably group energy, but keep your eye on the otherside in case your ghost is projecting energy or manifesting using that specific energy from you or one of your team members.

Cemetery View: Newark, New Jersey

2
Equivalent Tarot: High Priestess

Keyword: Cycles

May have an experience, but cannot prove it

How this investigation will affect you or your team personally:

This card has both a "high" and a "low." Seeing an apparition or having some sort of psychic experience puts one on a high, excited plane; however, not being able to prove it or having it disappear before the mind can truly grasp what has happened brings forth a grouchy state of mind. Yet someone can have a hunch that they might not be ready to blurt out — go ahead and say it because everything is going to be okay and the hunch is right on.

Special note: Someone around this situation feels a romantic tug... Who is it?

Cemetery View: Hollis, New Hampshire

3
Equivalent Tarot: The Empress

Keyword: Creation

Puzzling case, may need other professionals; protect team

How this investigation will affect you or your team personally:

For the most part, this is a positive experience card. It may take a while to solve the puzzles of this case, but the work involved will be worth the effort in the end. If you feel you are at a dead end, call in other professionals who might have other ideas to support your theories — demonologist/psychic/medium/empathic person. You will need to sit tight and wait for the outcome of some of your experiments. Just remember to always keep yourself and your teammates protected.

This is a card about progress though, and also points to someone who has knowledge of the arts and sciences or who may be closely connected to nature. A parent could be involved.

Cemetery View: Hollis, New Hampshire

4
Equivalent Tarot: The Emperor
Keyword: Power

Everyone feels in charge, even the client and ghost; aggressive emotions

How this investigation will affect you or your team personally:

This investigation may feel intimidating for many members because there will seem to continually be a movement of power through the group with each member feeling that he or she should be in charge (though oddly, this behavior is not one that fits normal behaviors for most members of the group). Even the client and the ghost will have a hand at trying to take over. It will all feel unsettling and later, the members of the team will all wonder why they felt such aggressive emotions. It will have been the haunting.

Keep the protection up. Watch for rivals. Let someone else make the first move. Bite your tongue if you feel the anger erupting, or if the words have already tumbled out, remind those around you that it wasn't you who felt compelled to lash out. The Devil made you do it.

Cemetery View: Northampton Cemetery, Massachusetts

5
Equivalent Tarot: Hierophant
Keyword: Believing

An obvious person to follow who always knows the right thing to do

How this investigation will affect you or your team personally:

The right thing to do will always present itself to this person in your group and you will instinctively know who this person is. Everyone else may be on the wrong path, but you can expect this person to know the score and how to stay on the path that will lead to success and safety. Best bet? Follow along. Take a moment to notice who this person is.

There may be an opportunity at the very end of this investigation that will prove to be exciting. Watch for it. If you miss it, that chance will be gone forever.

Consider the number 10 or 10th when this card comes up — save a 10th, 10 percent, 10th day of the month, 10th month, 10 something.

Cemetery View: Northampton Cemetery, Massachusetts

6
EQUIVALENT TAROT: LOVERS

Keyword: Union

Love interest or connection between two; some kind of joining

How this investigation will affect you or your team personally:

There is, of course, always the possibility of a love interest within the team or even between a client and a team member, two ghosts, or another coupling of some kind that will affect the investigation. This could also mean the connection of partners, the bringing on of new team members, or some other joining of two. At any rate, regardless of the two involved, make sure that all true intentions are on the table — and remember that no one is there to judge; you just need the facts to move forward.

Cemetery View: Trinity Church Graveyard, New York City

7
Equivalent Tarot: The Chariot

Keywords: Conflict & Resolution

Victory, celebration

How this investigation will affect you or your team personally:

Everybody is happy around this card because victory is at hand. Is that win on this side or the otherside?

There is the possibility of someone related to the investigation in a uniform — a positive encounter and a victory. A leader has emerged.

(Is someone thinking of a new car?)

There was hard work and everyone did their job well. A celebration was or is at hand. A warning comes that says: Just remember that everyone was part of that success and not to be too self-centered when stepping forward to take the just rewards. It is unknown whether this celebration was in the past and related to the haunting or is for the victory of the team. Either or both could be involved.

Whether you recognize it now or not, this investigation will be a milestone, not only for the group but also for your future cases.

Cemetery View: Trinity Church Graveyard, New York City

8
Equivalent Tarot: Justice

Keyword: Decisions

Keep detailed reports, clean evidence trails

How this investigation will affect you or your team personally:

It should be commonplace that your team make reports and keep track of evidence, but if this card is drawn, it is very important that everything is carefully reviewed and documented, for within that evidence lies an important truth. It could be missed if you are not diligent. Don't jump to conclusions or make something out of nothing. Let the evidence speak alone without any added theory. Stay calm and professional. Not only are you judging evidence, but the client is judging you. Your reputation is always on the line.

During the investigation, check and double check the operation of your equipment. You can't afford for any of it to be "down." Something of great importance to the case could be captured and you don't want to miss it. Pay special attention to video equipment.

Cemetery View: Milford, Connecticut

9
Equivalent Tarot: Hermit

Keyword: Seeking Truth

Allow an intuitive to be team leader; surprise in store

How this investigation will affect you or your team personally:

For this investigation, you should allow (or invite from another team) your psychic, medium, empathic to be lead investigator and to do most of the communicating. This is the person who will be able to get to the truth this time. Have a list of questions prepared so that your advisor can easily move from one to the next. EVPs are acceptable as long as carried out in a low-key way. Do not be surprised if you learn something surprising about the ghost.

If you are already on the investigation and draw this card, have your lead investigator drop back to become a formal observer and allow the person who is most psychically sensitive to step up. The observer should feed the sensitive questions in a written format with no one else speaking. Record the session.

Cemetery View: Boothbay, Maine

10
EQUIVALENT TAROT: WHEEL OF FORTUNE
Keyword: Fate

Stay focused, ignore the limelight; have an escape plan

How this investigation will affect you or your team personally:

At this time, all eyes seem to be on the team for the high-profile cases you have been taking or for some venture that has had, or will have, public appeal. Prepare well for your investigations and don't take your eyes off the case to bask in the limelight just yet. It's always best to keep your guard up, just in case.

There seems to be the warning to have an escape plan for a current or upcoming case. There is a risk with this case — someone could

get hurt, but luck is involved so just keep your eyes open. It could be as simple as tripping over debris and not ghost related at all, but the cards do not indicate how the "injury" arrives. Take all precautions. Make sure you have checked out the landscape prior to the investigation. If you have not done that and are already investigating at an unfamiliar location, make sure everyone has a flashlight that provides a wide beam. Watch the floor as well as what's in front of you.

This is a risk, luck, fate, change card, though, and everything is running in your favor as long as you take care (for as long as it lasts). Now would be the time to take a risk if you needed to rather than waiting for a better time. If your hedging on a case, deciding whether to take it or not, knowing that eventually you *will* take it, get it over with and say yes. No time like the present. Just be careful.

Cemetery View: Oak Ridge Cemetery, Passaic County, New Jersey

11
EQUIVALENT TAROT: STRENGTH
Keyword: Telepathy

Involve a psychic, animal power; team on same wavelength

How this investigation will affect you or your team personally:

This investigation may feel like a trip to the zoo to the team. You definitely feel the animal power, though there is nothing physical to warrant it. This would be a very good investigation to involve someone with psychic ability, for that person will be able to put some of these energies into context.

On a very good note, you will see that members of the team will be able to pick up on each other's thoughts without speaking,

The Paranormal Investigation Deck 73

with only a glance or hand motion. At the same time, be careful of mixed messages — varied members on the team might receive the same message, but perceive it differently, causing conflict.

There may be some destructive forces in this case that you will have to manage. The ghost involved may have mismanaged something in life that it is working out in death, and that is causing conflict on this side. If there is a way to calm the spirit and to explain why the death occurred (from a historic sense), the haunting could be stopped.

A "wild one" may be involved in this case. You may have to be a lion tamer!

Cemetery View: Oak Ridge Cemetery, Passaic County, New Jersey

12
Equivalent Tarot: The Hanged Man

Keyword: Crossroads

*Several visits for resolution;
need spiritual counselor for client*

How this investigation will affect you or your team personally:

An investigation where the spirit is at a crossroads may turn into several visits to actually move towards a conclusion, for it may take that long to resolve whatever issue the spirit is dealing with. The client, too, will need attention, and it may be wise to bring a spiritual counselor to work with that person or persons.

There may be a choice involved between two — two people, two relationships, two lifestyles, two something. The warning that goes with this is: Don't make the same mistake twice. Your dilemma is: Whose warning *is* this?

This spirit really is in a state of limbo and somehow needs to understand that letting go is the only way to have peace. Waiting for a rescue will not work — this spirit needs the team to help it move on.

Cemetery View: Oak Hill Cemetery, Nyack, New York

13
Equivalent Tarot: Death

Keyword: Change

Severing of a connection between the client and the otherside; may not be welcome

How this investigation will affect you or your team personally:

Change can be a difficult, but this change is not one that affects the team in a personal way. It is about the ghost or client and the severing of the connection between two worlds so that both can move on.

When this card turns up, the team needs to be cognizant of the fear that the client will feel about a painful or unwelcome change. Find out what the change is and, if you can, provide measures that will ease transitions and give spiritual explanations. If possible, include a spiritual person for counsel.

For the ghost, this is a card of conclusion. It is on its "last leg." This is the time for crossing over, leaving behind any significant hurt or wrongdoing, and making its way towards rebirth. It will be the team's responsibility to advise and convince the spirit of this.

Cemetery View: Oak Hill Cemetery, Nyack, New York

14
Equivalent Tarot: Temperance

Keyword: Miracles

Unreasonable request or expectations by client who requires a miracle

How this investigation will affect you or your team personally:

The team is wondering about all this talk of miracles: Why has the client even called for help? It feels like an unreasonable request and no one on the team believes it possible. There is a breakthrough, though, reminding us that there really are miracles. Use a dynamic approach for this investigation. Something that you have considered, but may have thought to be too "off the wall." It will be very much "on the wall" for this one. The client will be very impressed with the ghost equipment and enamored by the team. (Watch out for physical attractions — remember that people in extreme situations tend to have romantic connections to those who save them.)

Cemetery View: Boothbay Harbor, Maine

15
Equivalent Tarot: The Devil

Keyword: Trap

Stay alert and in groups of at least 2; violence not out of question, ghost attachment possible

How this investigation will affect you or your team personally:

This card can indicate traps for not only the client, but also the team or individual team members. It would be advisable to stay alert and to always stay in groups of two or more while investigating. Violence of some kind is not out of the question. There are mixed discussions about whether a ghost can follow an investigator home. True or not, this would be the time to be careful about it.

There is a control mechanism in place during this investigation that is unhealthy. It appears that the otherside has tethers to this side hooked to a specific thing or person. There also seems to be a lashing out that causes negative thinking and thought forms that affect those close by. Keep protective measures high.

Cemetery View: Boothbay Harbor, Maine

16
Equivalent Tarot: Tower

Keyword: Electricity

Literal reading of death by electricity, or a shock of some kind received or delivered

How this investigation will affect you or your team personally:

A literal reading of this card might indicate that a person died by electrocution or lightning or in a storm. However, it could just as easily mean that the death was a shock. It is possible, too, that there may have been a scandal and all that goes with a high-profile disgrace.

This could also mean that a structure has a negative attachment. It is said that some properties are inherently evil — that could be the case on this one if a person or ghost cannot be identified. Someone in your group should have a "flash" of insight that will help with this identification. Do not discount it, though it feels as if it is coming out of "left field." Regardless, major changes are happening and are alarming to all involved. There is a positive outcome after the "fall" however.

Cemetery View: New York City Marble Cemetery, New York City

17
Equivalent Tarot: Star
Keywords: High Hopes

Good reputation, burning the midnight oil

How this investigation will affect you or your team personally:

The team has a fantastic reputation—possibly all over the media and named in books (if not now, in the future) and is known for getting the job done. Often, members need to burn the midnight oil to keep that reputation.

In this investigation, reputation must be put aside. Keep your focus because the positive impressions are also coming from the otherside. Someone there is impressed as well and, though you may not get much physical evidence, information may come to you or a team member in a dream. Keep a dream log and discuss methods for remembering dreams.

The caution is that the spirit may be so enamoured with someone in the room (client or team) that it plans to stay connected. Put up protections. Even nice ghosts shouldn't attach to you.

Cemetery View: The Old Burying Ground, Cambridge, Massachusetts

18
EQUIVALENT TAROT: MOON

Keyword: Instincts

Keen insight, right on track with your thoughts and senses

How this investigation will affect you or your team personally:

You will be right-on with this investigation. If someone on the team has a thought, make sure they speak up — chances are they will be right because insight is keen at this time. People will be looking to the team for answers because they too can sense that what you are seeing and sensing is exactly on track.

It's possible that the case may revolve around something that happened in some kind of vehicle — meaning something that took a person from here to there (not necessarily a car). Possibly a romantic touch to the case in some fashion, too, though there is uncertainty whether it involves the client or the spirit. (Ask the client. Your hunch is probably correct.) There seems to be a mix of business and pleasure. An impulsive decision works out.

Cemetery View: The Old Burying Ground, Cambridge, Massachusetts

19
Equivalent Tarot: Sun

Keywords: Free Will

Open-minded client, freedom to explore all the possibilities

How this investigation will affect you or your team personally:

This card will tell you that each team member will feel the freedom to explore freely in this investigation without feeling tethered to the chains of tradition. The client will be open-minded and will accept all ideas no matter how bizarre as possibilities until proven otherwise.

Is there something new in your toolbox of equipment. Test it on this investigation. You won't find a better opportunity to see the positive aspects of its performance.

You're on the right track. Keep to the path you're on.

Cemetery View: The Granary Burying Ground, Boston, Massachusetts

20
Equivalent Tarot: Judgment

Keywords: Final Decisions

Clues offered: don't "spin" answers to suit beliefs; accept the evidence

How this investigation will affect you or your team personally:

This can be a frightening card to come up if the team is not ready to either speak the question or hear the answer. The cards give the clues to the outcome. Settle back and don't fight it or try to "spin" the outcome. Accept what you see.

A letter, e-mail, or phone call holds vital information and how you respond will give you control over progress. A surprise is involved; a mixed message becomes clear.

You may get good EVPs. This card indicates voices from the past—maybe a long-lost love. There may be a romantic entanglement involving the ghost. All good news in the end.

Cemetery View: The Granary Burying Ground, Boston, Massachusetts

21
Equivalent Tarot: World

Keywords: Rebirth

Reincarnation or residual haunting

How this investigation will affect you or your team personally:

This investigation may show a residual haunting. A spirit may be returning over and over to review a particular scene to gather or repeat in order to learn from it. This is often the case in times of war (i.e., the fields of Gettysburg, Pennsylvania), but can happen anywhere and during any scene.

There is a year around this card. Whether the ghost has been repeating the scene for a year at the client's expense or whether it will take a year to rid the client of the ghost is unsure. It appears that a love interest is involved and that the case will eventually have an optimistic conclusion, but it will take time.

Cemetery View: The Granary Burying Ground, Boston, Massachusetts

The Paranormal Client Deck

Using the Paranormal Client Deck

During the Client Interview

There are usually at least four instances when the client is approached by members of a paranormal research team. Once the client has contacted a team, there is most often a telephone interview, a face-to-face interview, a walk-through of the haunted property, and finally the investigation. Sometimes, other circumstances will vary the routine, but regardless, there are usually instances where reading cards cannot only give clarification for the team, but also assist the client.

The best usage of a card reading is during the face-to-face interview (before taking a walk-through, though sometimes done after the walk-through works just as well) where the client(s) are included in the participation. It acts as a good fact finder and will definitely bring information and personality from the client. You will find that once the reading is underway, the atmosphere will begin to lighten and the clients will usually become more vocal, remembering items they've forgotten but that may be imperative to the case. You will also find out if the client will be adversarial or not, which usually shows when the client displays negative behaviors at this time. This may indicate difficulties during your investigation (*forewarned is forearmed*, perhaps).

Before or After the Investigation

It is advisable to have the client at least present at a reading conducted before the investigation if not allowing their participation. Oftentimes, allowing them to participate is a good decision because any spirit at the property may be inclined to react more vivaciously if a known "entity" participates. (Remember to always record the readings.) There is no reason not to allow the client to participate in a reading after the investigation if it is conducted at the haunted location. Not only does it close the investigation for the team and places a protective barrier (with the right closing prayer), it does the same for the client.

Paranormal Client Deck Meanings

0
Equivalent Tarot: The Fool

Keywords: Starting Over

Some clients experience skepticism, but are willing to take a leap of faith

Understanding a Client:
This client is taking a leap of faith because there may be a tad bit of skepticism that only comes from uncertainty of this new situation, but once the "smoke and mirrors" in the client's eyes dissipate, the uncertainty disappears.

He or she is impressed by the science and conviction of a well-organized team and even is willing to participate should the need arise. In fact, there is a secret desire to become more intimately involved once the mechanics of ghost hunting is understood. You may be looking at a new ghost hunter in the making.

Having said that, remember that though the client has all the right "stuff," he or she is still an innocent beginner and needs to be mentored closely. This is not because of any mistake that could be made with the investigation, but rather in a manner of protection from any unwanted dissidents on the otherside who might find this person a vulnerable subject to plunder. A good practice when this card comes up would be to invite the client's interaction with the card reading, at least with the speculation points raised at this particular layout. The client may have "new eyes" to see things that the team may not have thought important.

Always consider the client as a part of your team.

Cemetery View: Sleepy Hollow Cemetery
Long Island, New York

1
EQUIVALENT TAROT: MAGICIAN

Keyword: Energy

Excited client, picking up on anomalies routinely; monitoring required, possible danger

Understanding a Client:
The client has been drawn into the situation like a moth to flame. He or she feels as though they are picking up on something that the spirit is thinking or saying — and may be seeing or feeling anomalies routinely. There is no fear here; it's almost as if there is a romantic pull. The client should be monitored closely for their own good. Danger could be near — not specifically from the ghost, but just from being involved with interactions from the otherside without any real knowledge of the otherside. Everyone on the team understands the consequences of working with the otherside without having the experience to do so. It's not always dangerous, but it can turn in a second.

Cemetery View: Sleepy Hollow Cemetery, Long Island, New York

2
Equivalent Tarot: High Priestess

Keyword: Cycles

Client's emotions high, has many experiences; wants team to believe

Understanding a Client:

The client, who has had many experiences with this particular anomaly, will be psyched up and ready for action. The consensus is that this is the only way to prepare for what is to happen. Emotions will be high and the client will attempt to pump up the team so that they will not miss an experience that can be there and gone in seconds.

However, the team must stay calm and professional, though there is a definite urge to follow suit. This is indeed an exciting case. Excitement can cause things to be missed, exaggerated, or misdiagnosed. Slow and steady.

Cemetery View: Poughkeepsie Rural Cemetery, New York

3
Equivalent Tarot: The Empress
Keyword: Creation

Child involvement; possible romantic relationship around the case

Understanding a Client:
This client is very, very serious and there may be children involved — either on this side or the other. Either way, the client has a firm commitment that may affect a child. There may be a romantic relationship around this case as well.

Cemetery View: Ho-Ho-Kus Cemetery, New Jersey

4
Equivalent Tarot: The Emperor

Keyword: Power

All feel uneasy upon entering location; aggression, power loss/power gain

Understanding a Client:

The client knows that help is needed due to family and visitor changes. There is the sensation that each person wants power because everyone feels a loss of it. Children may have problems in school, depression, and aggression. Adults register problems in relationships, have depression, and money issues. Everyone uneasy, touchy, negative.

If such an atmosphere has not developed, warn the client to watch for it—it may be a sign of escalating issues. Also, some people may be more prone to feeling negative effects and others may have better protective fields. For them, these things may not become a problem, but for those who are not protected or who have mild natures, the assault can be considerable.

Cemetery View: Near Barryville, New York

5
Equivalent Tarot: Hierophant

Keyword: Believing

Bothersome person not allowing investigation to move forward

Understanding a Client:

This person may annoy you (because he or she is always right and tends to talk a great deal about spiritual and religious matters), but regardless of that, you know you need to look at both sides when investigating. Just take a step back and explain the scientific procedures. This will give the person a reason to understand, but do this in a respectful way and remember that this person needs help. It would be best to give this person a job. Teach the client about EMF and then have him or her take readings for the team, making sure that they are recording their findings on a graph of the location. This will most likely solve a problem. Remember not to insult your client.

Cemetery View: Near Barryville, New York

6
Equivalent Tarot: Lovers
Keyword: Union

A connection of two, possible love interest; dig deeper.

Understanding a Client:

The law of two is possibly reflected for the client. There is a connection to either the ghost, the team, or some other person or thing that will affect the success of the investigation and the team's interaction with the case. The strongest probability here is that there is a love interest connected to the client. It could be a severing through the death of a loved one or a relationship on this side that negatively affects the spirit. If you don't notice one, dig deeper.

Cemetery View: Westwood, New Jersey

7
Equivalent Tarot: The Chariot

Keywords: Conflict & Resolution

Client feels part of the team — a good thing

Understanding a Client:

The client feels the victory as well as the team and feels as though he or she is part of the team. Allow that for it hurts no one to care for the living in this way. Remember that you would not have had this success had you not had this client.

This client has good coping skills, and the determination to follow through with any assignment that you leave with him or her to take care of once the team leaves.

Cemetery View: The Granary Burying Ground, Boston, Massachusetts

8
Equivalent Tarot: Justice

Keyword: Decisions

Something hidden, details left out; don't jump to conclusions

Understanding a Client:

It's possible that your client knows something that he or she is not telling or that something is known that he or she does not think is important, but is. The client must be convinced to tell the entire story without leaving out any details, no matter how small. You should not jump to any conclusions until you hear the whole story, no matter how tempted you are to do so.

One thing to be cautious of is permissions. Make sure you have the appropriate authority to conduct the kind of investigation you have planned; it would be best to have that in writing. It never hurts to be careful.

Cemetery View: Westwood, New Jersey

9
Equivalent Tarot: Hermit

Keywords: Seeking Truth

*Client may know ghost or
more than letting on*

Understanding a Client:
There's a possibility that the client may know the ghost intimately and not even know it. Although the client will listen closely to all the evidence collected, the answers collected will be nothing new. The client may leave to hide out, running away from a perceived problem. Though there is distance involved — between life and death — a journey seems to be bringing your client right back to where things started many years ago.

Cemetery View: Lyon, France

10
EQUIVALENT TAROT: WHEEL OF FORTUNE

Keyword: Fate

Client going in circles, pulled by the otherside; understanding helps a lot

Understanding a Client:

The client has been going in circles; one minute up, the next down, and not understanding the emotional roller-coaster. For the first time he or she will begin to realize that the pull from the otherside is having an effect on the energies of the human condition. It will be much easier now for the client, no matter how the investigation goes. Knowing is the first key to making things right.

The good news is that the client has the ability to be the catalyst for making the case go positive or negative, just by understanding the problem. The team's job is to be convincing enough to provide the client with reason for a positive conclusion — and to remain positive.

11
EQUIVALENT TAROT: STRENGTH

Keyword: Telepathy

Spirit protecting client; invite spiritual advisor

Understanding a Client:

It's clear to the team that the spirit would like to protect this client and does not like to see specific people around the property. The client knows this as well, and though interested in having a free-will life, does not want to "hurt" the spirit's feelings. It would be best to have a spiritual advisor to counsel the client. The idea would be for everyone involved to understand truly that living is for those alive and not for the deceased. Moving on is imperative for the spirit.

Cemetery View: Paris, France

12
EQUIVALENT TAROT: THE HANGED MAN

Keyword: Crossroads

Choice involving 2 for client, may involve spirit; do not discount what client reveals

Understanding a Client:

The client has a choice to make that seems to involve two of something. This seems to correlate directly with the interaction with the spirit and may be why the spirit was drawn to the situation if it is one that is not known to the client. The client is likely to make the right choice and this will be helpful to the spirit, so do not discount what the client reveals or any opinion voiced.

Allowing the client to stay with the team during the investigation in this case may be a good idea. Prompt the client regarding protocol and possibly allow a job that might allow him or her a focus. It should be something that is enjoyable rather than taking notes. (EMF is always a good choice if you have an extra meter.)

13
Equivalent Tarot: Death
Keyword: Change

Client fears being alone once spirit leaves; much grief, difficult moving through it

Understanding a Client:

The client does realize that the spirit must go and that he or she will be left behind, but there is fear of being alone. There is no way to move around grief. One must move through it. It would be good to have in the team's arsenal something that assists clients with the steps of grief. Having a spiritual counselor on hand would be beneficial, otherwise someone who has the ability to empathize should spend some time with the client.

Cemetery View: Poughkeepsie Rural Cemetery, New York

14
Equivalent Tarot: Temperance

Keyword: Miracles

May be a fragrance relating to spirit, anomaly now an obsession; client may want spirit to stay

Understanding a Client:

The client is smelling a fragrance related to the spirit, a physical proof that the ghost exists. What has started as an anomaly has turned into an obsession and may be unhealthy. The client will want the spirit to stay.

The team should have a policy about this prior to any investigations. What goals will the team have when taking on an investigation? Will the team be there to serve what's best for the client or for the ghost/spirit?

(Remember, when you take on an investigation, you begin with the client. If you have a desire to do what is best for the spirit at all costs — even if detrimental to the client — the client should know this up front.)

15
EQUIVALENT TAROT: THE DEVIL

Keyword: Trap

Chaotic client, feeling doom; spiritual counseling needed

Understanding a Client:

The client will most likely be feeling chaotic. The sensation of doom will permeate every room of the location and a feeling of invasion will be evident on the client's face. The client feels as though he or she has been tethered to the devil. It will be difficult to pull the client from this abyss. A spiritual advisor should be available.

It should be noted, too, that team members could also be taken in by the same trap that the client has entered. Set up extra protections, and remember that after an investigation, sometimes the haunting will increase and this will be frightening for the client. There should be an emergency plan in place to handle such incidents. Do not leave your client "high and dry." Advise them appropriately and truthfully of things that could happen.

Cemetery View: Warwick, New York

16
Equivalent Tarot: Tower

Keyword: Electricity

Client either physically shocked or shocked by something seen

Understanding the Client:

The client has been shocked in some manner. If not by the haunting, possibly by something that has happened around an electrical appliance. Or maybe something seen on television or heard on the radio that has affected the anomalies on the property. The client too could have been involved with a storm or lightning.

Regardless, there is a stormy presence that requires attention, but has not been able to get a point across. The client has a feeling that is "right on" about the message, but a part is missing. It will be the team's job to lead the investigation to that missing part.

Cemetery View: Paris, France

17
EQUIVALENT TAROT: STAR

Keywords: High Hopes

Client is expecting miracles; discuss what can and can't be done up front

Understanding the Client:

Clients expect miracles from this team. They've watched a lot of television programs and read a lot of books. Not realizing that there is much "down time" when investigating paranormal activity, they want answers right *now*. Therefore, it is imperative that there be a script developed that explains what actually can be done as opposed to what clients believe can be done (i.e., what their misconceptions can be). Put on your persuasive hat, but don't knock the television shows or books in the world because you will be knocking the client's intellect by suggesting that he or she does not have the ability to understand *real* paranormal activity. Whether you believe that or not, remember you are there to educate, to find a problem, and solve it. It does no one good to hear you beat a drum.

Cemetery View: Paris, France

18
Equivalent Tarot: Moon

Keyword: Instincts

Give leeway for the client to digest what is uncovered, as these things aren't easy to understand

Understanding the Client:
Do be careful with your client's feelings. Yes, you are right about your feelings that the client's thoughts and desires regarding the case are not exactly the way things really are in the paranormal world, but if those agendas happen to be less than positive, take care not to attack. Not everyone understands why they think and believe the things they do. Give people some leeway to understand what it is they are about to witness. The fact that you know what the truth is will be enough at this time. No need for the world to know. (This is really hard to do, but hold the tongue. After all, do you *really* know the truth?)

Cemetery View: Cave Hill Cemetery, Louisville, Kentucky

19
Equivalent Tarot: Sun

Keywords: Free Will

Clients are open-minded about evidence and happy to know what they are up against

Understanding the Client:
Pulling this card to understand the client will show that he or she is open-minded about the evidence or ideas that will be uncovered by the investigation. There will be a welcome change in the family's demeanor as they no longer struggle with the unknown, but begin to understand what they are up against.

This is the best kind of client to have because they will truly listen to what you have to say and will follow any directions that you have for them. Indebted to you for helping them, you may have found a training ground for future new member sessions (just don't abuse the privilege).

Cemetery View: Cave Hill Cemetery, Louisville, Kentucky

20
EQUIVALENT TAROT: JUDGMENT

Keywords: Final Decisions

What outcome does the client want? How does that compare to what is?

Understanding the Client:
There's not much to think about here. The question was clear when you sat down to talk with the client. The answer, too, is clear in the cards. This is a "matter-of-fact" kind of client. He or she will require proof and solid evidence. Though willing to look at psychic phenomena and will even admit to feeling some of it, the only true test will be the ghost equipment. The final presentation after the investigation will be as important as the actual investigation. Be prepared to leave copies of your reports (no typos please). If you goof this one up, expect to see a rating on the Internet — not that the client is vindictive; that's not the case, but *reputable* is part of this client's name. Do your homework.

Cemetery View: Cave Hill Cemetery, Louisville, Kentucky

21
EQUIVALENT TAROT: WORLD

Keywords: Rebirth

Spirit either known or attached to client; sad or uncomfortable.

Understanding the Client:

The client is still learning and this go-round seems to be of great interest because it involves the otherside. It may be that the spirit involved with the client is known to the client or is in some way attached to the client. It is not, however, a negative attachment, but rather a sad and uncomfortable arrangement.

Has there been a death in the family or of a close friend? It may not have even happened recently. It could be that a deceased acquaintance is about to reincarnate and has come to say goodbye via a haunting, or there may be a spirit just passing by who stopped by for a quick visit. This will not be a long haunting. After a period of time, this ghost will just ... fly away.

Cemetery View: Sleepy Hollow Cemetery, Long Island, New York

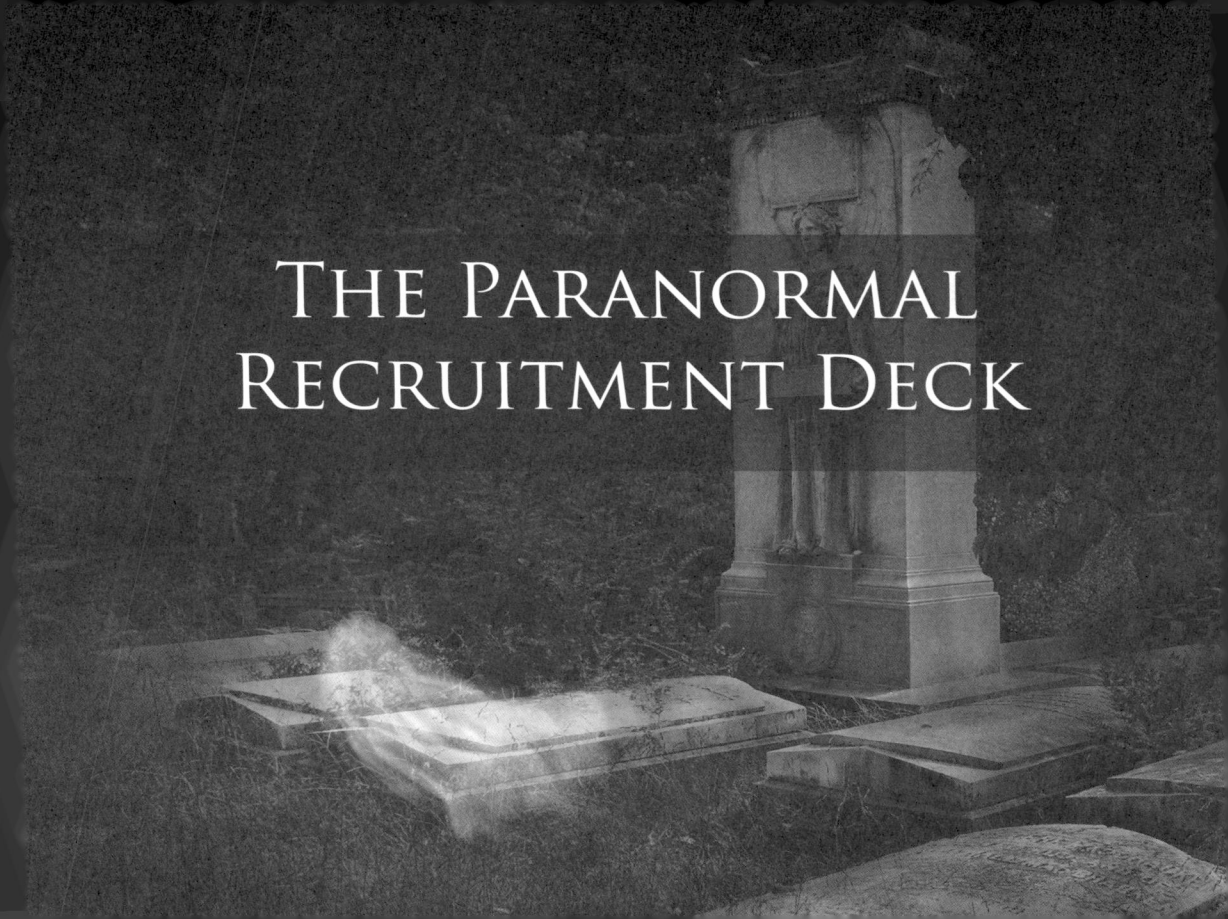

How to Use the Recruitment Deck

Bringing new members into your paranormal team is always a trying task because just like any job interview, people are at their very best when being considered for any position they really want. Since this is a volunteer position (in most cases), the sentiment of doing one's best is tripled. It is likely that the person wanting to join the group is highly motivated and excited about the opportunity. This excitement can sometimes overshadow true abilities — or lack thereof. I've talked with many a group who have brought in a team member only to find out that the fit was not what they'd hoped it would be. Yes, there would been an application and interview process and possibly even a probationary period, but let's face it, that probationary period is rough on a group and it is so tough to tell a nice person who just doesn't fit, that they... well, they don't fit! So, let the cards help just a bit.

Prior to the face-to-face interview, it is best to use the Recruitment deck and, with another trusted team member, discuss your new candidate. It is here that you will come up with questions that need to be considered as you move forward. What problems are you likely to face with this person? What position would be a best fit? Consider making a jump-off list of recruitment questions to use for all recruitment practices.

At the face-to-face interview, after you've taken your application and gone through your normal selection process, use the Major Arcana deck to loosen the candidate up. The person will, of course, be nervous. Let the first reading be for fun. Come up with questions that allow the person to get to know you as well as for you to get to know him or her. Then move on from there. Having already used the Recruitment deck and knowing the pitfalls and stumbling blocks of the person as well as possible strengths, you will be able to maneuver your discussion via the cards before you. The idea is for you to "bring out" the person so that you can see him or her in a personal light, revealing thoughts, feelings, abilities, nuances, — the things that are not revealed during a mere questioning.

> **Tip:** If there is time and you feel comfortable, you can also add the Investigative deck to the Major Arcana deck, and through the cards, make up a mock scenario involving the prospective new member. In this way, you can find out how well he or she will think and act during an investigation. (It is best to use this strategy with a team member who is proficient at reading the cards and interviewing new members.)

Paranormal Recruitment Deck Meanings

0
Equivalent Tarot: The Fool

Keywords: Starting Over

Go-getter; they need specific focus or will involve him/herself in all aspects

Interviewing a potential team member:
    This is a happy-go-lucky individual who will do what it takes (over and over if needed) to get to the bottom of a situation. The only thing to watch when inviting this person onto an investigative team is the tendency for him or

her to want to be involved in all aspects of the investigation at once, rather than focus on his or her own assignment. This is not done in a negative way, rather this person really wants to help and thinks that by doing it all, it can only help. A calming hand is needed to "handle" this team member. Let him know that, yes, he will be learning everything, but one job at a time.

The idea at play here is that this new recruit is like a sponge and experience is the water to fill the mind. Consequences are not in the forefront unfortunately, and if the team leader does not lend that calming influence, the group might find that the risks being taken or the added tasks that the recruit offers forth (oftentimes in front of a client) puts the entire mission at an influx of work not needed.

But this is not to be taken as a negative, rather just as a warning to be the calming "teacher" to a new student. This recruit will spawn rainbows under the right influences, for his or her nature is pure in the desire to be there to help everyone needing it.

Make sure you have a job for this person. I'll say it again. A job. Give this person a job!

Cemetery View: Miner's Cemetery,
Franklin, New Jersey

1
EQUIVALENT TAROT: MAGICIAN

Keyword: Energy

Looks at things via an esoteric level; very knowledgeable, skilled

Interviewing a potential team member:

This person is very knowledgeable and practices his or her skills religiously. There is probably a good understanding of psychic abilities and the varied religions that practice earth faiths. The person may be a member of a New Age or pagan religion or have an interest in such things. This is a very good person to have on a team because they look at things from a more esoteric level.

Cemetery View: Warwick, New York

2
Equivalent Tarot: High Priestess

Keyword: Cycles

High positive energy, take-over type; have a specific plan for this person

Interviewing a potential team member:
Have a specific interview plan for this person, otherwise the interview will be directed by the potential member and not you. The person is highly energetic and can draw you into that energy quickly. It is positive energy and the person is a good candidate, but you should never go away from an interview and later say, "Gee, I didn't get answers to half my questions, because I never had the chance to ask them."

Cemetery View: Gettysburg, Pennsylvania

3
EQUIVALENT TAROT: THE EMPRESS

Keyword: Creation

Creative, open-minded, lots of ideas

Interviewing a potential team member:
This is a creative person with endless ideas. There is a great interest in scientific procedures of ghost hunting, but not so heavily sought that they do not understand that there is another esoteric side to the field that we can learn from. Open-minded, sometimes more so than those on your team who are science-oriented would like, but having that balancing counterweight is a good thing.

Cemetery View: Gettysburg, Pennsylvania

4
Equivalent Tarot: The Emperor

Keyword: Power

Cautious, does not let down guard easily; may fool (even you)

Interviewing a potential team member:
You will notice that this person is very cautious and will wait to see what your opinions are before presenting his or her own, and then those responses will align suspiciously close to yours. It's not that this person is not telling the truth; more that he or she is practicing interviewing skills rather than letting down their guard to be genuine. This has been taught by the media. Use the cards to loosen things up. Talk about investigations that are not privacy related. Get this person talking! Otherwise, you could've stayed home and talked to your mirror!

Cemetery View: Gettysburg, Pennsylvania

5
Equivalent Tarot: Hierophant
Keyword: Believing

Always right

Interviewing a potential team member:
Yes, you can see right away that this person is always right. It's good to be always right, isn't it? Are you up for it? (Not being sarcastic here — this person *is* always right!)

Cemetery View: Hatfield, Massachusetts

6
Equivalent Tarot: Lovers

Keyword: Union

Check person out well, don't be fooled by a pretty face; be sure they're truthful

Interviewing a potential team member:
Remember that this is a love card and ghost hunting is not about love (well not when it comes to recruiting, anyway). Be on your toes, check this person out well, and don't be fooled by a "pretty face." Do tell your true intentions, but make sure that the person is being truthful with you.

Cemetery View: Knowlton, New Jersey

7
Equivalent Tarot: The Chariot

Keywords: Conflict and Resolution

Serious and leader material

Interviewing a potential team member:
The person you are interviewing takes this opportunity very seriously. He or she is well-dressed (and may even be in a uniform of sorts) and could very well be leader material. If you need someone to back you up in a pinch, this is the one.

Cemetery View: Harper Cemetery, Harpers Ferry, West Virginia

8
EQUIVALENT TAROT: JUSTICE

Keyword: Decisions

Have a probationary period, agreements; consider honesty

Interviewing a potential team member:
Question your decision to invite this person onto your team. If you do invite them, consider having a probationary period. It's possible that this person may cut corners during investigations and that honesty is not an important part of his or her personality. At the very least, draw up an agreement for new members that allows you to "fire" at will.

Cemetery View: Harper Cemetery, Harpers Ferry, West Virginia

9
EQUIVALENT TAROT: HERMIT

Keywords: Seeking Truth

Psychic ability? Add this person for balance if he/she meets other criteria

Interviewing a potential team member:

If the person you are interviewing has psychic ability, it is wise to consider adding him or her to your team (if your other criteria is met). Having a balanced team involving both the scientific and spiritual is important. Having two such folks is even better, so that they can be "checks" for each other.

Cemetery View: Harper Cemetery, Harpers Ferry, West Virginia

10
Equivalent Tarot: Wheel of Fortune

Keyword: Fate

Risk, could go either way

Interviewing a potential team member:
A certain amount of risk with this potential team member, but it might be okay. It could go either way as far as a good fit goes, but the positive just might outweigh the negative. Play the odds as you see fit.

Cemetery View: Green Mount Cemetery, Baltimore, Maryland

11
Equivalent Tarot: Strength

Keyword: Telepathy

Strong character, honest, responsible

Interviewing a potential team member:

This candidate will require a spirit of co-operation as there is a strong sense of self and responsibility. Not a bad thing, but the person will do what is necessary to make sure his or her opinion is heard regardless of the situation or whether right or wrong. Strong character, and very honest and true.

Cemetery View: Green Mount Cemetery, Baltimore, Maryland

12
Equivalent Tarot: The Hanged Man
Keyword: Crossroads

Be careful, don't make same mistake twice; sleep on it

Interviewing a potential team member:

Before you make a decision about this particular person, sleep on it and then wait 24 hours. Do not make the same mistake twice. There are issues here that will put you on the same road that was traveled before with another member that ended badly. Be mindful of your teams' needs.

Cemetery View: Green Mount Cemetery, Baltimore, Maryland

13
Equivalent Tarot: Death

Keyword: Change

Bring in new talent, fill needs not space

Interviewing a potential team member:
It's time to shake up your team by bringing in some new talent. Revamp your interview process and needs. What do you really need? What slows your progress now? Find people to fill the needs instead of space.

Cemetery View: Green Mount Cemetery, Baltimore, Maryland

14
Equivalent Tarot: Temperance
Keyword: Miracles

Decide where this person will fit into the team — or pass on them

Interviewing a potential team member:
As you are interviewing this candidate, remember that you will be needing to realign your team into a changed entity as they learn new tasks and as you bring new people in. People will need to be matched in personality and ability for investigation, leaders placed in charged of mini teams, and dynamic approaches identified and implemented. Will this person fit into the plan? If not, pass. At least for now.

Cemetery View: Mt. Olivet Cemetery, Frederick, Maryland

15
EQUIVALENT TAROT: THE DEVIL

Keyword: Trap

No openings right now

Interviewing a potential team member:
Cancel the interview — there are no openings at the present time.

Cemetery View: Mt. Olivet Cemetery, Frederick, Maryland

16
Equivalent Tarot: Tower

Keyword: Electricity

Take care, this member could get hurt on an investigation; protection

Interviewing a potential team member:
Be careful. This team member could get hurt during a future investigation. It could be shocking — or via any of the afore-mentioned electrical things. If this person comes on-board, take special precautions, and do let the person know that this card was pulled in relation to their recruitment so that they, too, can be responsible for their own protective rituals. The truth is, it may not be a physical hurt at all, but an emotional occurrence. This is unclear, except that it will not be the member's fault.

Cemetery View: Princeton Baptist Graveyard, Princeton, New Jersey

17
Equivalent Tarot: Star

Keywords: High Hopes

Smooth communicator, good with clients

Interviewing a potential team member:
More good team members are needed. Put together a good interview process. This one will be a star on your team and will be well-liked by clients. Sending this person in for initial client interviews will pave the way for smooth investigations. Grab this person before he or she gets away.

Cemetery View: Oak Ridge Cemetery, Passaic County, New Jersey

18
Equivalent Tarot: Moon

Keyword: Instincts

Base decisions on intuition; keep thoughts to yourself during the interview

Interviewing a potential team member:

If you've drawn this card prior to an interview, keep your knowledge to yourself as these interviews for new members begin. Do not tip your hand. If you do, the potential team member will surely try to block or enhance themselves with white lies and other countermeasures. Just keep things light and airy. See where they take you. Then make your decision based on your own intuition. You will be correct in your assessments.

Cemetery View: Green-Wood Cemetery, Brooklyn, New York

19
Equivalent Tarot: Sun

Keywords: Free Will

Positive outlook, open-minded; good at reviewing evidence

Interviewing a potential team member:

This person as a team member will be open-minded and willing to accept the opinions of other team members. Also willing to participate in experiments to prove or disprove theories, there is a positive outlook towards change and exploration.

Cemetery View: Green-Wood Cemetery, Brooklyn, New York

20
Equivalent Tarot: Judgment

Keywords: Final Decisions

You will know if the candidate is right; if not, be gentle

Interviewing a potential team member:
As in "Understanding the Client," the same is true while interviewing for a team member. You will see immediately whether this potential member has worth for your group. Be gentle if the decision shows to be negative.

Cemetery View: Sleepy Hollow Cemetery, Long Island, New York

21
Equivalent Tarot: World

Keywords: Rebirth

Been in another group? Ask the question; still a good candidate

Interviewing a potential team member:
 This potential member may have been in another group prior to applying to your group. There may not have necessarily been a negative reason to his or her leaving that group, but the question should be asked if that information was not offered. This new appointment will be a rebirth for this person and a positive involvement. A good candidate.

Cemetery View: Sleepy Hollow Cemetery, Long Island, New York

THE CEMETERY VIEWS

Initially, I thought that Stuart Schneider's beautiful cemetery art was a lovely enhancement to this tool kit that would give it the feel that we in the paranormal field love. What I didn't realize was that it would go much deeper. Most of us who have worked with ghost investigations have at one time or another taken our services, training groups, or interests to the cemeteries of the world. There are varied theories about them. Some say that all are haunted, others say they are not. Regardless, most all of us love them for one reason or another. We can wonder about the ancestors who have passed, the names and dates showing on crumbled stone, or the massive monoliths giving the illusion of greatness even in death. Those same things are evident on these card cemetery views.

What has happened here is just as these photos have found a place in print, they are also imprinted in spiritual ways. There are those individuals who will be connecting to the artwork as well as the messages. Still others will be drawn to the specific locations of the cemeteries. This will be especially true for those groups who live near the cemeteries shown. I've seen psychics view the cards and then hold them, eyes closed, and see the full cemetery, understanding the spirits that roam there. I've seen empathic individuals shiver as they've looked upon the cemetery plots so cryptically displayed.

So do not leave the images behind as you use these cards. They have value and can add to the spirit of your investigations. Not everyone will find connection in this way, but those who do, will be greatly surprised at the depth of the messages they receive.

For your convenience of location and further cemetery research, I have listed the cemeteries here along with their location (if I have them) and the card I have them attached to.

As I mentioned, there will be those in your group who have psychic bents, like empathy or other intuitive skills in varied areas. These people may find that the cemetery views have visual significance for them. Though the scenes were not chosen to match any particular message, it is well known in the mind/body/spirit

Major Arcana Deck Views

Cemetery	Location	Deck	Card
Old South Church Cemetery	Bergenfield, New Jersey	Major Arcana	0 Fool
The Woodside Cemetery	Dumont, New Jersey	Major Arcana	1 Magician
The Woodside Cemetery	Dumont, New Jersey	Major Arcana	2 High Priestess
Parkesburg Cemetery	Parkesburg, Pennsylvania	Major Arcana	3 Empress
(Name Unavailable)	Gettysburg, Pennsylvania	Major Arcana	4 Emperor
Saugerties Cemetery	New York	Major Arcana	5 Hierophant
Good Hill Cemetery	Kent, Connecticut	Major Arcana	6 Lovers
Green-Wood Cemetery	Brooklyn, New York	Major Arcana	7 Chariot
Green-Wood Cemetery	Brooklyn, New York	Major Arcana	8 Strength
Green-Wood Cemetery	Brooklyn, New York	Major Arcana	9 Hermit
Green-Wood Cemetery	Brooklyn, New York	Major Arcana	10 Wheel of Fortune
Green-Wood Cemetery	Brooklyn, New York	Major Arcana	11 Justice
Green-Wood Cemetery	Brooklyn, New York	Major Arcana	12 Hanged Man
(Name Unavailable)	Boothbay, Maine	Major Arcana	13 Death
(Name Unavailable)	Boothbay, Maine	Major Arcana	14 Temperance
(Name Unavailable)	Fallsington, Pennsylvania	Major Arcana	15 Devil
(Name Unavailable)	Fallsington, Pennsylvania	Major Arcana	16 Tower
(Name Unavailable)	Jerome, Arizona	Major Arcana	17 Star
(Name Unavailable)	Jerome, Arizona	Major Arcana	18 Moon
(Name Unavailable)	Jerome, Arizona	Major Arcana	19 Sun
(Name Unavailable)	Boothbay, Maine	Major Arcana	20 Judgment
(Name Unavailable)	Edgecomb, Maine	Major Arcana	21 World

Paranormal Investigation Deck Views

Cemetery	Location	Deck	Card
Sleepy Hollow Cemetery	Long Island, New York	Investigation	0
(Name Unavailable)	Newark, New Jersey	Investigation	1
(Name Unavailable)	Hollis, New Hampshire	Investigation	2
(Name Unavailable)	Hollis, New Hampshire	Investigation	3
Northampton Cemetery	Massachusetts	Investigation	4
Northampton Cemetery	Massachusetts	Investigation	5
Trinity Church Graveyard	New York City	Investigation	6
Trinity Church Graveyard	New York City	Investigation	7
(Name Unavailable)	Milford, Connecticut	Investigation	8
(Name Unavailable)	Boothbay, Maine	Investigation	9
Oak Ridge Cemetery	Passaic County, New Jersey	Investigation	10
Oak Ridge Cemetery	Passaic County, New Jersey	Investigation	11
Oak Hill Cemetery	Nyack, New York	Investigation	12
Oak Hill Cemetery	Nyack, New York	Investigation	13
(Name Unavailable)	Boothbay Harbor, Maine	Investigation	14
(Name Unavailable)	Boothbay Harbor, Maine	Investigation	15
New York City Marble Cemetery	New York City	Investigation	16
Old Burying Ground Cambridge	Massachusetts	Investigation	17
The Old Burying Ground	Massachusetts	Investigation	18
The Granary Burying Ground	Boston, Massachusetts	Investigation	19
The Granary Burying Ground	Boston, Massachusetts	Investigation	20
The Granary Burying Ground	Boston, Massachusetts	Investigation	21

Paranormal Client Deck Views

Cemetery	Location	Deck	Card
Sleepy Hollow Cemetery	Long Island, New York	Client	0
Sleepy Hollow Cemetery	Long Island, New York	Client	1
Poughkeepsie Rural Cemetery	New York	Client	2
Ho-Ho-Kus Cemetery	New Jersey	Client	3
(Name Unavailable)	Near Barryville, New York	Client	4
(Name Unavailable)	Near Barryville, New York	Client	5
(Name Unavailable)	Westwood, New Jersey	Client	6
The Granary Burying Ground	Boston, Massachusetts	Client	7
(Name Unavailable)	Westwood, New Jersey	Client	8
(Name Unavailable)	Lyon, France	Client	9
Poughkeepsie Rural Cemetery	New York	Client	10
(Name Unavailable)	Paris, France	Client	11
(Name Unavailable)	Paris, France	Client	12
Poughkeepsie Rural Cemetery	New York	Client	13
Dale Cemetery	Ossining, New York	Client	14
(Name Unavailable)	Warwick, New York	Client	15
(Name Unavailable)	Paris, France	Client	16
(Name Unavailable)	Paris, France	Client	17
Cave Hill Cemetery	Louisville, Kentucky	Client	18
Cave Hill Cemetery	Louisville, Kentucky	Client	19
Cave Hill Cemetery	Louisville, Kentucky	Client	20
Sleepy Hollow Cemetery	Long Island, New York	Client	21

140 The Cemetery Views

Recruitment Cemetery Views

Cemetery	Location	Deck	Card
Miner's Cemetery	Franklin, New Jersey	Recruitment	0
(Name Unavailable)	Warwick, New York	Recruitment	1
(Name Unavailable)	Gettysburg, Pennsylvania	Recruitment	2
(Name Unavailable)	Gettysburg, Pennsylvania	Recruitment	3
(Name Unavailable)	Gettysburg, Pennsylvania	Recruitment	4
(Name Unavailable)	Hatfield, Massachusetts	Recruitment	5
(Name Unavailable)	Knowlton, New Jersey	Recruitment	6
Harper Cemetery	Harpers Ferry, West Virginia	Recruitment	7
Harper Cemetery	Harpers Ferry, West Virginia	Recruitment	8
Green Mount Cemetery	Baltimore, Maryland	Recruitment	9
Green Mount Cemetery	Baltimore, Maryland	Recruitment	10
Green Mount Cemetery	Baltimore, Maryland	Recruitment	11
Green Mount Cemetery	Baltimore, Maryland	Recruitment	12
Green Mount Cemetery	Baltimore, Maryland	Recruitment	13
Mt. Olivet Cemetery	Frederick, Maryland	Recruitment	14
Mt. Olivet Cemetery	Frederick, Maryland	Recruitment	15
Princeton Baptist Graveyard	Princeton, New Jersey	Recruitment	16
Oak Ridge Cemetery	Passaic County, New Jersey	Recruitment	17
Green-Wood Cemetery	Brooklyn, New York	Recruitment	18
Green-Wood Cemetery	Brooklyn, New York	Recruitment	19
Sleepy Hollow Cemetery	Long Island, New York	Recruitment	20
Sleepy Hollow Cemetery	Long Island, New York	Recruitment	21

circles that the universe places things exactly where they are supposed to be for the results that are supposed to take place at any given time. This would indicate that the views for each card do then have specific meaning to some *one* for some *thing*.

These people having this affinity should look at the card images closely in a meditation pose and try to envision themselves inside the scene. They should ask themselves how the image makes them feel, who they see, what they hear or smell, and what their interpretation in relation to the investigation is. You may be surprised to find that there is more to the scene than first imagined. There are clues. (Everyone in the group should try this and a discussion should take place because no one knows until they try just how in-tuned they are to the visual side of the cards and to these images in particular.)

There are those in your group who may wish to use the cemetery views without the messages on the reverse sides of the cards. These folks rely entirely on intuition and the messages received from the *otherside* or the universe. This I've seen accomplished in a séance-like session, where one card is placed on the table in front of the team member as he or she concentrates on the scene while going into meditation mode. At some point, impressions will begin to flow as the image is viewed. The spirit may actually talk about the image or may talk about something else, but these impressions will be sent to the person, who will then air them to the group. In some investigative groups, the cards are passed then to the next person who repeats the pattern, and so on until everyone has had a chance to meditate on a card and receive impressions. Between each person, the impressions are discussed.

This is a perfect way to practice intuitive development. If you have not participated in this kind of exercise before, it is difficult to just say things that come to mind in a group setting, but once that little hurdle is crossed, you will find that intuitive sparks from these images will come rapidly and a connection to the otherside will become natural. Do not worry if you do not receive impressions when it becomes your turn to look at the card. Not everyone receives intuition in the same way. Keep trying, though, because this can become a practiced skill that develops over time. Additionally, please say what is on your mind regardless of how strange or silly you think it may sound. You'll be sorry if you don't because you will find that it was truly intuition and someone else may say the same thing! Practicing this exercise during monthly meetings (not at interviews, investigations, or recruitments), at training sessions, or when alone is an excellent way to improve the intuitive sensitivities and thereby improve the abilities that will be needed on actual investigations.

Of course, visiting the actual cemeteries where the photographs were taken should be a great deal of fun and especially conducting investigations at some of the locations. The stories associated with the images can be found in Stuart's *Ghosts in the Cemetery* and *Ghosts in the Cemetery II: Farther Afield*. Be sure to let us know about your results!

Dowsing

Dowsing has been used in ghost investigations for as long as people have been investigating ghosts and is considered one of the more esoteric tools in the bag of tricks that investigators use. The dowsing category sports both pendulums and dowsing rods, including homemade or slick store-bought models of each.

We chose to include the dowsing rods with this kit because we have found that they are the dowsing tool *least likely* to be discriminated against as not compatible to other scientific gadget-type tools — since people did (and still do) in fact use rods (in the form of a forked stick or rods) for finding water in days past. There was an actual confirmed use for it beyond paranormal divination.

Today, as far as the dowsing rods go, there are two veins of thought. One mirrors times past advising us that the rods do well for identifying locations for water and also other things such as minerals or gemstones, objects, and (for the purposes of this book) gravesites. This is especially helpful to a group who is searching for a grave that is unmarked, but to which there is other evidence indicating that the location is in a particular area, specific locale unknown. Those groups who use the rods in this fashion may not believe that there are connections to other methods of dowsing, i.e., like as with the pendulum or that the rods can be used to answer questions (as with the K-2 meter).

The other vein of thought is that the dowsing rods do indeed provide a specific method of divination and provide answers to questions by the movement of the arms giving *yes*, *no*, and *uncertain* replies to questions asked. This belief, I have found, is held by most psychics (but not all) and all animal communicators I have interviewed. It is also one that I subscribe to, since I have personally seen the results by a psychic/ghost investigator and have had results myself (via animal communication) and energy experiments. Other psychic mediums I've seen using the rods believe that they are talking directly to the spirit involved. (I have done this with the pendulum, so that particular belief, I find acceptable, if not always safe.)

Regardless of the interpretation of usage, the question of those watching often is: *Where does the movement or information gathered from the movement come from?* These are good questions, for no one truly knows. The psychics and animal communicators who believe that the tool is used for divination believe in most cases that information comes from one's spirit guides or higher self, both topics of broad interest when it comes to self-awareness and mind, body, spiritual thinking. Those who believe that the rods are used as simply a way to locate places or objects think the same in some cases, but in other situations think that the rods are moved by involuntary motor actions of the person holding the implement who has gleaned some form of internal knowledge of the location via other natural abilities. That's a hard one for me to phantom, considering my own usage of the dowsing rods, and since my natural ability to find most things seems lacking. However, in the world of the paranormal, I find it best to doubt nothing. Still others advise that there is a direct connection to the spirit in question. I have also seen, what I believe to be true, this in action.

To make matters easy for the users of the dowsing rods included in this kit, you have two separate ways of using them based on what you or your group choose to believe.

Finding Objects or Locations

If you believe that dowsing rods only find locations or objects, the following methods should be used:

1. Hold one of the L-shaped wired rods loosely in each hand about three to four inches apart.
2. Walk forward with your mind centered on what it is you are looking for. (Make sure that you do not have others close by, as another's energy can interfere with your own, giving you a false reading.)
3. When the two rods cross in an *X* formation, you have found your object or location.

Divination with Dowsing Rods

To use the rods as a way to answer questions from a spirit/ghost:

1. Establish by other means that a ghost or spirit is nearby. (Use EMF equipment, note temperature changes, physical phenomena, EVP, etc.)
2. Hold one of the L-shaped wired rods loosely in each hand about three to four inches apart.
3. Ask the rods to show you what a *yes* response looks like. (The rods will *usually* cross in an *X* fashion, but could show another movement.)
4. Ask the rods to show you what a *no* response looks like. (The rods will *usually* uncross and widen so that the wire moves far apart, but could show another movement.)
5. Ask questions. (Have your session videotaped or recorded with someone reciting results or someone taking notes.)

What Else Can You Do With Dowsing?

I didn't include a pendulum in this kit because creating a personalized one is incredibly easy and having two forms of dowsing in one kit is overkill.

Early on, I was always enthralled with the beautiful pendulums that could be found in stores. For years I had used a specific one that *called* to me from a small mind/body/spirit shop, but then…and I was crushed…I lost it. When I consulted the cards, and my intuition, and psychics I knew, and every other trick I had, it was clear — I wasn't going to find my trusty long-held pendulum. It was gone.

I started looking for another one that spoke to me and I was becoming desperate. Days were moving into weeks and I'd not found one that jumped off the store shelves saying, "Buy me!" I was using a little homemade one that I'd been given in an animal communications class thrown together with a piece of yarn and a nut that fits overtop a screw thingy — you

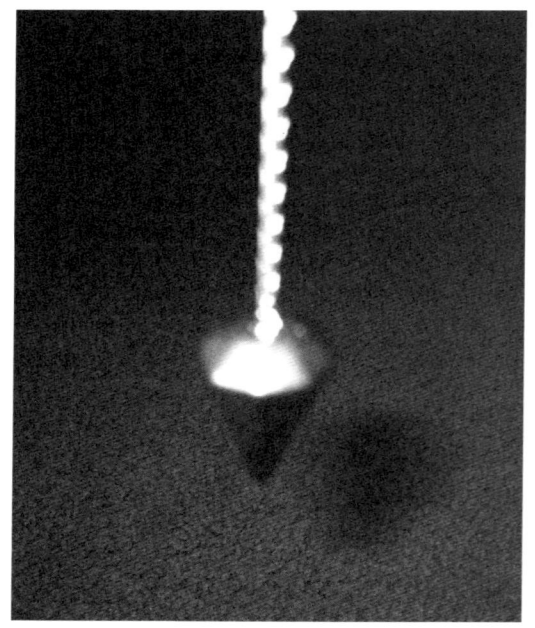

can tell I'm not a fix-it kind of person. I knew from years of dowsing that anything would work. It all had to do with spirit for me and I could make a telephone receiver on a spiral cord swing like a pendulum if I wanted to. (I'm not kidding — it's spirit.)

Anyway, I began to use a necklace my daughter had given me for Christmas. The next thing I knew, a year had gone by and that had become my pendulum until one day something jumped out at me from (are you ready?) an Avon catalog. (Yes, men, I know you're not likely to look at an Avon book, but this just gives you an idea that things come to you in strange places and most anything will work — even a bobble.) I'd found my new pendulum for $15 dollars: a perfectly weighted teardrop-effect necklace. It had my name on it.

Author's Postscript: *The day after I wrote this section detailing how a person did not have to buy a specific store-bought pendulum, the store-bought pendulum that had been my first, which I had loved and lost a year prior, was sitting in the middle of my bathroom floor when I woke up one morning. I had not put it there. My husband didn't even know what it was. The little bag it had been in when I'd lost it was not with it, but the pendulum was there.*

I have had items go missing before and then show up within the next day or two (see my prior ghost books), but never something for this long. My digital camera went missing from an investigation at Gettysburg two weekends ago; I wonder if that will show up... Ah, the paranormal.

> The point is: Have all the tools you can for your kit. Make them if you have to. Gadgets don't have to be expensive to work.

Conclusion

To conclude, let me say that everyone knows that what we know about the paranormal world is changing all the time. What was once thought to be paranormal or supernatural is now natural with more and more phenomena occurring everyday.

Will it be very long before intuition becomes the standard way to identify truth? How will one spark these intuitive thoughts? Certainly, finding a connection to brain function is one way and brainstorming power brought to the surface by using cards as an indicator is a sure way to spur that function.

Use these four decks as a jump-off point to your own growth in the paranormal world. Dowse your way to knowledge of the world beyond. Fairly soon, I'm certain that what once *was*, will be no more, and what we *see*, will be far more natural than paranormal. We can only be ready for it if we test our intuitive abilities right along with our scientific minds.

No time like the present!

I hope you enjoy this kit and come up with even more ways to use the tools provided here, for I feel that we have only scratched the surface.

For now, we say:

Ghostly regards!

Dinah Roseberry
Stuart Schneider

Appendix

Do's and Don'ts When Using the Kit Under Ghostly Circumstances

Don't Spit At Your Clients or Members!

Caution:

When using your reading skills with new members or clients (especially clients), take care not to insult them.

Just because the card has a negative connotation, this does not mean that you should smack them in the face with it. Note the negative in your mind and then put a positive spin on it. Of course, if you don't want new members or don't care about your client's feelings (or whether you get referrals or good media press), well that's another story.

Truth is important. Yes. I can hear some of you — truth, no matter what the cost. I've talked to many people who feel this way, but never let it be said that someone in your group has no compassion, no common sense, no people skills, and no right being in the business. Always be the professional. No one was ever hurt doing the right thing and, while being professional does mean telling the truth, it does not mean insults or know-it-all behavior.

Trial Runs Save Face

Do let people know that you are trying out this new tool kit for the first six to ten investigations or interviews — or about six months. It takes that long to see how it will work for your group. Allow several members of your group to try it out. Use it within the group before using it in public. If you have a bad experience with it, troubleshoot — just like you do with your other tools. Find out why, what went wrong, how can it be fixed. Don't expect to be a professional reader the first time out of the gate, although some (and maybe most) will. This tool is as much about your own ability to talk and interpret as it is about investigation. You cannot rely on physical evidence with the cards. Your mind becomes the catalyst for success. That takes time.

Use the kit outside of your investigations during practice sessions, monthly meetings, or at home. Pass it from member to member to play with during down times. The more you use it, the better the results you will have during a live investigation.

Hooking Concepts Saves Time

At first, if there is someone in your group who has Tarot or oracle card skills, it would make sense to allow that person to take the lead. The training time will go quickly. If not, choose someone who is in a sales or public relations profession who is comfortable hooking concepts together and speaking in front of people as the beginning leader. Make sure, though, that it is firmly stated that speaking skills are not required to succeed. People should not be intimidated by the cards. Remember that the entire group can be part of the discussion and can chime in when using the cards during an investigation. No one

Brainstorming

A person who is psychic is helpful, but remember that you do not need to be psychic to use this method. It is more about brainstorming and bringing people out of their shells in an intuitive fashion than having psychic connections. But I must say that the more you use this program, the more psychic intuitive occurrences you will have. (Ask anyone who reads cards routinely. This will improve your intuition.)

More Ways than One to Use the Decks

The interesting thing about these decks is that you do not need to be together in a group to use them. They can be used via conference call, the Internet, or a regular phone call, too. If a group has more than one kit, decks can be combined with interesting results. There can be two dealers pulling cards for separate individuals with same or different questions. Separate areas in an investigation can have readings going on at the same time. The sky is the limit.

Protection – Never Forget It!

Another reminder because it's important. Never forget the beginning protective prayer or the closing prayer/rituals. It is imperative to your health and those who sit with you.

Shut the Door!

Should you find yourself with a client or a prospective new member, and the cards, your own intuition, and outside influences are so explosively negative or suspect that you want to shut the session down, simply mention that the cards have refused to cooperate for some reason and that you will try a bit later (then don't!). Regardless of how you stop, take a few seconds, in your mind, to strengthen your protection in case that negativity is attacking. Do not allow your client or member to take that from you. Put your hand up to stop them from talking, close your eyes, and **shut that door**. It's for everyone's protection. Liken this to an Ouija session gone wrong. It can happen and you must protect those participating.

Clarifiers

Do try using the cards with other divination tools, like the rods, pendulum, or runes. I have had good reports regarding these combinations. I often use the dowsing rods or a pendulum as a clarifier after the cards are laid down and the client asks something that I don't see clearly in the cards I've drawn. (If you are using another form to clarify your cards, however, please research the proper usage so that you employ it safely. Especially if you are considering using an Ouija Board. (I do not encourage Ouija usage because most people have not thoroughly researched it and it has been known to cause havoc beyond what can be controlled. It is for professionals only, so be sure you remember to be professional around it.)

Sharing Dowsing

Although I have found that anyone seems to be able to pick up the dowsing rods without worrying about who was using them prior, if you use a pendulum, you should not share it. The energy with it should be yours.

Other Ways To Use The Decks

The Major Arcana Tarot Deck

The Majors Tarot deck, though slanted here to work with the paranormal ghost investigative world, can easily be used in any situation you apply it to, be it your home life, the office world, or any question that is pertinent enough for you to ask. Learning the Majors is a great way to introduce one's self to the entire seventy-eight cards that make up the traditional Tarot deck.

The entire 78-card deck can also be employed in the paranormal world, but is often daunting to those who don't know it well at the onset. It does answer questions in much more depth and gives detailed clues that the Majors-only deck will not supply. Still, if there happens to be someone in your group who has experience in reading the Tarot, allow that person to introduce you first to this deck and then to routinely add more cards from the full deck until the group has learned all 78 cards — *if* that is your goal. It is by no means necessary to be successful with this kit.

Having said this, using a full 78-card deck during an investigation is sometimes not the most practical way to handle a reading. It can take a quick and easy intuitive snapshot of a scene and make it complicated. You will find that those in your group who have more of a science leaning will begin to fidget, not liking where the cards take them or the time it takes to get there. Time and energy could be wasted and, at the worst, this could sway some in the group from ever trying to use the cards again. A full reading using 78 cards to choose and read from can be consuming and investigators like to be on the move, so it makes sense to have a full disclosure discussion prior to trying an experiment like this.

Giving Meat to a Reading

Don't forget that using the Majors deck as a Wild Card piece is a fantastic way to give "meat" to your readings in any one of the other decks. You can either mix the cards into the deck or shuffle them separately and add one Tarot card to each card of one of the other decks that you lay out. Then the cards can be read together.

> For example: If one of the cards you choose for recruiting a new member is the 11 STRENGTH card stating that the person is honest and responsible and then the Tarot card you lay on top is the HERMIT card saying that the person is intimidated by ghost equipment, what does this tell you? You get depth by using the Major Tarot card to clarify the Recruitment card.

You are also within your rights to look to the person you are reading for to ask them, "Does this make sense to you?" If they say yes, you may ask them why. Then you will learn how this affects your group. If no, you should just move on to the next card, or you may add another clarifier card (from the Tarot pile or the regular deck pile — you call all the shots).

The Paranormal Investigative Deck

Just like with EVP at the investigations, the investigative deck can also enhance ITC (Instrumental Transcommunications) sessions. Again, it works best when the session is being recorded so that both the ITC words are caught on tape as well as the interaction that the team has with the cards. The cards should be read slowly and individually. The question should be asked and while the ITC equipment is providing words, a card should be drawn. When the ITC stops, the card should be read by a team member to show comparison or connection.

Another way to use the cards in either the EVP or ITC sessions is just to turn one card over at a time and say the main keyword, pausing to allow the spirit to respond. Then connect the card's word to the words received on EVP or ITC. The interpretations can be very revealing or interesting. This too can be a way to include the client in your investigation and this may increase the evidence you take away, since it is likely that the spirits involved are already accustomed to interacting with said client.

You will be able to use the cards with most of the new interactive voice equipment that people are discovering everyday with just a little bit of thought.

The Paranormal Recruitment and Client Deck

Both of these decks can be taken outside the ghost environs and used in the corporate (or nonprofit) world with just a bit of slanting. Job interviewing (prior to interviews — not *on* interviews because no matter how "today" the corporate world likes to boast they are, they haven't made it this far yet) is a great place to use these decks, mixed together and clarified with the Majors Tarot (pull the shades and lock the door), but do be sure to remember that the cards are merely indicators of questions you need to consider and prepare for and will not give you specific absolutes for your hiring decisions — no "drop-dead" answers in most cases. The cards require interpretation and interaction. You need to add your brain power, common sense, and analytical skills to the mix. There's a knack to decision-making that no card display can prepare you for entirely.

One Final Equipment Note

Please note, that though not all items used in ghost investigations, or even mentioned here, are included in this kit, if you intend to use them, they should be researched fully. This should include *any* other tool you choose to employ — new or old. Why? Not only will people ask you about them, but when you invite other members to join your group, they may have them already and plan to use them.

Little by little you can add to your equipment when your finances allow (not all equipment is cheap, though some of it is coming down in price and most people have voice recorders, computers, and video equipment these days).

Also know that if you plan to use equipment that requires electric power, there is setup time involved and most always a drain of power from paranormal anomalies. You'll need to have someone on-board who not only understands all the equipment, but also will be responsible for setup and take down. The time commitment during an investigation can be considerable for this.

The Good News and The Bad News

The bad news is that oftentimes equipment will fail to work during a ghost investigation. This usually comes in the form of energy draining batteries, cameras being hurled off tripods, and any number of crazy things that we investigators have seen.

The good news is, if all the techie stuff fails and all the batteries are dead, your cards and dowsing rods will still work right along with your intuitive mind.

"And that's all she wrote."